Mastering Manga Studio 5

An extensive, fun, and practical guide to streamlining your comic-making workflow using Manga Studio 5

Liz Staley

PUBLISHING

BIRMINGHAM - MUMBAI

Mastering Manga Studio 5

First published: September 2013

Production Reference: 1170913

Published by Packt Publishing Ltd.
Livery Place
35 Livery Street
Birmingham B3 2PB, UK.

ISBN 978-1-84969-768-2

www.packtpub.com

Cover Image by Elizabeth Ann Staley (dynamitecandy@gmail.com)

Credits

Author
Liz Staley

Reviewers
Heldrad

Mark Egan

Carlos Naizir (Rizian Larc)

Mohammed Ali Vakil

Acquisition Editor
Saleem Ahmed

Lead Technical Editor
Balaji Naidu

Technical Editors
Vrinda Nitesh Bhosale

Anita Nayak

Rohit Kumar Singh

Project Coordinator
Kranti Berde

Proofreaders
Kelly Hutchinson

Bernadette Watkins

Indexers
Tejal Soni

Mariammal Chettiyar

Priya Subramani

Production Coordinator
Aparna Bhagat

Cover Work
Aparna Bhagat

About the Author

Liz Staley first started writing and illustrating stories when she was young. Her first novel was written by hand in a Marble composition book in middle school. In high school, she began to write another novel, the first book of that series was then published ten years later as *The Hinomoto Rebellion*. In 2010, she began her first long-form story webcomic, *Adrastus*. The giant robot love letter in comic form ignited a strong passion for comics as a story-telling form.

Aside from drawing and writing stories, Liz also loves to play role-playing games, read, watch cartoons from the 80s and 90s, and go for long walks. She lives in Western Pennsylvania with her very supportive husband, Byron.

Many special thanks to Smith Micro for their assistance with software and planning for this book. And to Julie Devin Minter for helping with proofreading and questions.

About the Reviewers

Heldrad is a freelance webcomic artist who has been posting her works online since 2004. She writes and draws her own stories, and lately, has begun self-publishing her comics in local conventions and participating in international Manga contests such as The Morning International Comic Competition and the Shounen Jump Manga Competition.

Mark Egan is a web cartoonist based in Oslo, Norway. He is an Irish expat, and originally comes from the Dublin region of Ireland, but has since lived in China as an English teacher before settling in Oslo.

He graduated from Griffith College, Dublin with a BSc degree in Computer Science in 2004, and following his time in China, began a career in the telecoms industry in Ireland, starting with work as a call center agent. He later progressed to technical roles prior to the economic downturn in Ireland, after which he migrated to Norway, where he continues to live and work.

Having been actively cartooning since 2003, he focuses on producing Manga-style webcomics. His main works of note are *Back Office*, an office comedy based in a call-center and *Bata Neart*, a 'magical girl' web-manga set in Ireland.

Both comics are published online at `rawrtacular.com`, which is the main portal of his studio "RAWRtacular Productions".

Carlos Naizir, also known by his pen name Rizian Larc, is a graphic designer, freelance illustrator, and comic book artist from Bogota, Colombia. He has been working in Manga-style illustrations and comics since the beginning of 2012, and one of his most significant works is the webcomic series *Ereggia*.

Mohammed Ali Vakil is the founder & creative director of Sufi Studios. Though an accountant by profession, in 2010 he found his soul work to be in drawing spiritual comics. He's the author of two comic books—*40 Sufi Comics* and *The Wise Fool of Baghdad*—both of which have been nominated for awards. You can get to know more about his works at www.suficomics.com. He lives with his family in Bangalore, India.

www.PacktPub.com

Support files, eBooks, discount offers and more

You might want to visit www.PacktPub.com for support files and downloads related to your book.

Did you know that Packt offers eBook versions of every book published, with PDF and ePub files available? You can upgrade to the eBook version at www.PacktPub.com and as a print book customer, you are entitled to a discount on the eBook copy. Get in touch with us at service@packtpub.com for more details.

At www.PacktPub.com, you can also read a collection of free technical articles, sign up for a range of free newsletters and receive exclusive discounts and offers on Packt books and eBooks.

http://PacktLib.PacktPub.com

Do you need instant solutions to your IT questions? PacktLib is Packt's online digital book library. Here, you can access, read and search across Packt's entire library of books.

Why Subscribe?
- Fully searchable across every book published by Packt
- Copy and paste, print and bookmark content
- On demand and accessible via web browser

Free Access for Packt account holders

If you have an account with Packt at www.PacktPub.com, you can use this to access PacktLib today and view nine entirely free books. Simply use your login credentials for immediate access.

Table of Contents

Preface

Welcome to *Mastering Manga Studio 5*! You're probably wondering just what this book is going to be about, and what we mean when we say that this will help you master Manga Studio 5. `Dictionary.com` defines a master as "a person with the ability or power to use, control, or dispose of something". Well, by the end of this book, you are going to be able to use the features of Manga Studio 5. You're going to be able to take control of your workflow and your productivity so that you can make your comics and illustrations even faster than before. And you're going to be able to dispose of the features in the program that don't suit your needs so that they're no longer in your way.

It's my job to show you the best time-saving features of the best program that I have ever used for art. That is exactly how I feel about this software, by the way! I've used lots of drawing software in my life, and Manga Studio is, far and away, my favorite one. Especially Manga Studio 5, which has even made me like coloring my comics because of its easy to use brushes that mimic natural media.

If you illustrate, draw comics, or just like to draw in general, I think that you'll love Manga Studio just as much as I do. Especially once you see all the cool things that it can do. It's more intuitive than most graphics software out there, and is infinitely customizable for the way that you want to work. As you're going to discover in the chapters of this book, you can customize all of your drawing and painting tools, rearrange the workspace to fit the way that you draw, create and save custom page sizes and layouts for comic frames, make word balloons with ease, and run actions that will do multi-step, tedious processes for you at the touch of a button.

So if any of this sounds exciting and just what you need to get the most out of your drawing time, you're probably going to love this software. I can't stop singing its praises quite enough, and it was my passion for this software that brought you the book you are currently reading.

What this book covers

Chapter 1, Getting Familiar with the Story Features, deals with using the story editor to set up custom page sizes, multi-page setups, and two-page spreads.

Chapter 2, The Right Tools for the Job, deals with making custom pencils, inking pens, paint brushes, and importing and exporting tools.

Chapter 3, Palettes of a Different Color, deals with using color palettes and making your own palettes.

Chapter 4, Setting up Your Space, deals with setting up custom workspaces, saving those spaces, and switching between different setups for different tasks.

Chapter 5, Living in a Material World, deals with navigating and searching materials, editing and using existing materials, and making custom materials.

Chapter 6, It's Only a (3D) Model, deals with using the 3D options of Manga Studio, including pre-set poses, characters, creating custom poses, and importing models.

Chapter 7, Ready! Set! Action!, deals with playing and recording actions to speed up repetitive processes in your project, such as resizing batches of pages or setting up layers.

Chapter 8, Rulers and Speech Balloons, deals with using the ruler and speech balloon tools of Manga Studio. It includes the special rulers, such as perspective and concentric circles, as well as how to use the speech balloon tools to make custom balloons.

Chapter 9, Putting It All Together! Drawing and Inking, deals with making a multi-page comic file and making a custom material for the panel layouts. Then we'll be drawing using custom tools, and using 3D models to help with character poses.

Chapter 10, Finishing Touches, deals with using screentones and doing comic book style coloring using blending modes, the lasso selection tool, and the gradient tools. We will also explore a few special effects techniques, such as reflections and using patterns.

Appendix, Recommended Reading, provides a list of further references.

What you need for this book

In order to complete the exercises in this book, you will need:

- Manga Studio 5 (EX Recommended to complete all exercises)
- A computer capable of running Manga Studio 5

Also recommended is a graphics tablet, such as a Wacom brand tablet.

Since this book is for intermediate Manga users, much of it assumes that you already have a graphics tablet. If you haven't heard of a graphics tablet before, I recommend that you pick one up! A tablet is an input device usually consisting of a board and a pen, called a stylus, which allows you to draw directly on the computer with a more natural feel. Wacom is the most popular brand, but there are many other brands out there. Most tablets do not have a screen in them so you do have to get used to some disconnect as you are not looking directly at your hand while drawing. However there are options out in the market today that do incorporate a screen, so that you can draw while looking directly at the tablet.

There are also some older tablet PC laptops that allow you to draw and have pressure sensitivity right on the laptop screen. Most of this book was written on one of those, actually. I currently use a Gateway C-141X Convertible Tablet PC that I purchased.

Who this book is for

This is not a book for beginning Manga Studio users. I'm going to show you some of the basic features and how to use them, but I'm going to assume that you have some familiarity with the program, especially where to find the basic features. If you have never ever opened a digital art program before, this book is going to be a great help to you once you get the basics down. It might even help you figure the basics out if you're one of those people who like to learn software by pressing the buttons and seeing what they do. (This is how I like to learn programs, for the most part.) But this book won't explain what a layer is, or what the pencil tool is.

This is also not a book about how to draw comics. There are a lot of those out there, and I'll recommend some of my favorite ones in *Chapter 10, Finishing Touches*. But this is not going to be a drawing instruction book itself. In *Chapter 9, Putting It All Together! Drawing and Inking*, and *Chapter 10, Finishing Touches*, I do give some general drawing and coloring insights that I've gathered over the years, as they pertain to the information being covered in that section. But this won't show you how to draw your favorite Manga character or teach you perspective drawing. Maybe one day I can write a book like that, but this one concentrates on the software and how it can help you save time on the illustrations you're currently doing. (Thus, giving you more time to further your skills by getting more practice in!)

Conventions

In this book, you will find a number of styles of text that distinguish between different kinds of information. Here are some examples of these styles, and an explanation of their meaning.

Code words in text, database table names, folder names, filenames, file extensions, pathnames, dummy URLs, user input, and Twitter handles are shown as follows: "A save dialog box will come up, and by default our file name will be Sketching Pencil.sut."

New terms and **important words** are shown in bold. Words that you see on the screen, in menus or dialog boxes for example, appear in the text like this: "Click on the **Add new settings** button and a new entry will be created in our list of settings."

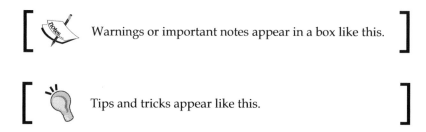

Warnings or important notes appear in a box like this.

Tips and tricks appear like this.

Reader feedback

Feedback from our readers is always welcome. Let us know what you think about this book—what you liked or may have disliked. Reader feedback is important for us to develop titles that you really get the most out of.

To send us general feedback, simply send an e-mail to feedback@packtpub.com, and mention the book title via the subject of your message.

If there is a topic that you have expertise in and you are interested in either writing or contributing to a book, see our author guide on www.packtpub.com/authors.

Customer support

Now that you are the proud owner of a Packt book, we have a number of things to help you to get the most from your purchase.

Downloading the color images of this book

We also provide you a PDF file that has color images of the screenshots used in this book. You can download this file from `http://www.packtpub.com/sites/default/files/downloads/7682OT_Images.PDF`.

Errata

Although we have taken every care to ensure the accuracy of our content, mistakes do happen. If you find a mistake in one of our books—maybe a mistake in the text or the code—we would be grateful if you would report this to us. By doing so, you can save other readers from frustration and help us improve subsequent versions of this book. If you find any errata, please report them by visiting `http://www.packtpub.com/submit-errata`, selecting your book, clicking on the **errata submission form** link, and entering the details of your errata. Once your errata are verified, your submission will be accepted and the errata will be uploaded on our website, or added to any list of existing errata, under the Errata section of that title. Any existing errata can be viewed by selecting your title from `http://www.packtpub.com/support`.

Piracy

Piracy of copyright material on the Internet is an ongoing problem across all media. At Packt, we take the protection of our copyright and licenses very seriously. If you come across any illegal copies of our works, in any form, on the Internet, please provide us with the location address or website name immediately so that we can pursue a remedy.

Please contact us at `copyright@packtpub.com` with a link to the suspected pirated material.

We appreciate your help in protecting our authors, and our ability to bring you valuable content.

Questions

You can contact us at `questions@packtpub.com` if you are having a problem with any aspect of the book, and we will do our best to address it.

1

Getting Familiar with the Story Features

Manga Studio 5 is a great all-around drawing software. But it's primarily a comic creation software, and as such the Multiple Pages feature is its bread and butter. The Page Manager tab functions like a book, allowing you to see zoomed-out versions of all the pages in your comic at once, open them individually, drag-and-drop them to new locations, and add or delete pages from your story at will. It's the thumbnail view of your story — the digital equivalent of having your pages laid out on index cards and shuffling them around as you please. It's a CMC file that points to individual image files of your pages in one convenient location so that you no longer have to keep track of separate files, like in other graphics programs.

In this chapter we are going to learn the following:

- Making a new story file
- Creating and working with custom page templates
- Saving custom page templates
- Navigating the Story tab
- Organizing pages
- Viewing options
- Easy text entry with the Story Editor mode
- Changing font face and size

Let's get started!

Creating a new file

In order to make a new story, navigate to **File | New** (or press *Ctrl+N*), or click on the new icon on your toolbar.

Once you've done that, the **New** dialog box will open. Make sure that the **Manga draft settings(O)** and **Multiple pages** checkboxes are selected. As you can see, we have quite a lot of options to play with here, so let's go over them.

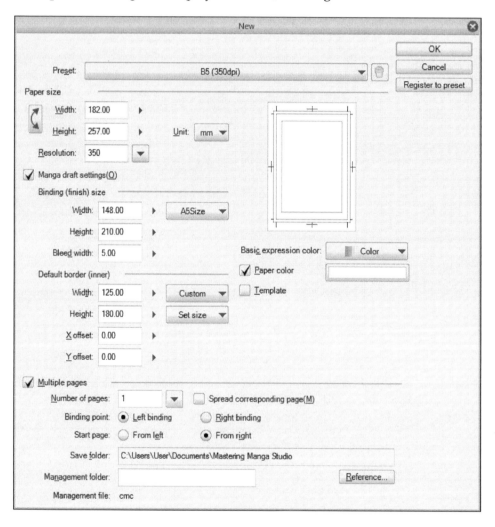

The **Preset** drop-down menu has common paper sizes used in the production of comics. It also has some other sizes, such as postcard and common web resolution sizes. What size and dpi setting you use is up to you and the specifications of your book printer.

My rule is to always plan to print, even if you're just thinking of doing a webcomic and have no ambitions to do so when you first start off. You never know when you might have a huge hit on your hands and suddenly get thousands of people screaming for you to make books. Or you might just decide that you really want to see your work in print! Set up correctly from the start and you'll save yourself a lot of work — and headaches later.

Print resolution is at least 300 dpi. The higher you can go on the dpi though, the crisper your work will look when it's printed. Most of the preset sizes in Manga Studio are already set to 350 dpi. If your computer can handle going higher, to about 600 dpi or so, then it's suggested that you do so, especially if you will be printing your work in black and white. High resolution is great for black-and-white work and produces nice, crisp lines.

Creating and saving a custom page template

The standard size for a newspaper strip is 4 1/16 by 13 inches (34.29 cm x 11.43 cm). We're making the width and height slightly larger than our finished size because we want our active drawing area to be 4 1/16 by 13 inches, and we need to account for the binding size and default border.

Want to have a long strip down instead of across? Or set a regular page size to landscape format instead of portrait? Simply click on the arrows to the left of the **Width** and **Height** fields to flip them!

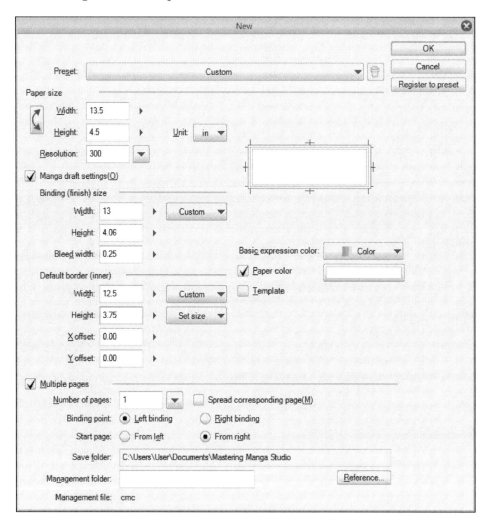

The **Binding (finish) size** is the final size of our page once the bleed is accounted for.

A bleed in printing is when the image goes off the page. In order to achieve this bleed, you must produce your artwork at a size larger than the final printed size, and draw to the edge of the canvas. When your work is printed, the excess at the edge will then be cut off, so don't put anything important near the bleed area!

Most printers require a bleed of at least one-eighth of an inch all the way around. So if you're going to be printing your comics in a 6 by 9 inch format, you will want to set your page size to 6.25 by 9.25 inches to compensate for the bleed. If you already have a printer in mind, be sure to get their printing specifications before you start drawing so that you can set your pages up correctly. It will save you time and a lot of headache in the end!

The **Default border (inner)** is the interior margin of the page. For most printers you should leave at least a quarter of an inch all the way around the edge inside which the important elements (such as text) stay, so that they're not cut off in the printing process.

The **X offset** and **Y offset** options for the basic frame will move the guides horizontally when the **X offset** value is adjusted and vertically for the **Y offset** value. Handy if you need a larger margin in the center of pages to account for a book's gutter, or if you wish to have a larger margin at the bottom or top of a page—say for text at the bottom or top with the comic title and author information.

Since we wanted our finished paper size to be 13 by 4 1/16 inches, under the **Binding (finish) size** field we're going to enter 13 and 4.06 inches (33.02 cm x 10.31 cm). The bleed will be an eighth of an inch on each side, so 16 should be close enough. Now, to achieve a bit of a gutter between the finished edges of our pages and the sides of our panels, set the basic frame to 12.5 by 3.75 inches (31.75 by 9.53 cm) and we have the dimensions of our drawing all set up. There are still a few more options on this screen to address though.

The **Basic expression color** option allows you to set the color mode for your entire file. It defaults to **Color**, but you can also select **Monochrome** and **Gray** from the drop-down menu. If you are creating a comic that will be in color, leave the setting on **Color**. For grayscale comics, use the **Gray** option. If you are creating a pure black-and-white comic, with no shades of gray included, then select the **Monochrome** option.

The **Paper color** option allows you to change the color of your base canvas. Since this can also be changed any time during the drawing process, I usually leave this white when I'm doing basic sketching, and then change it when I'm coloring. The drawing and coloring processes will be covered in *Chapter 9, Putting It All Together! Drawing and Inking*, and *Chapter 10, Finishing Touches*.

The **Template** checkbox allows you to pick a frame template material from the Materials library (covered more thoroughly in *Chapter 5, Living in a Material World*) to automatically place in your new file. There are many pre-set templates to choose from in Manga Studio 5. Checking this box will bring up the **Template** dialog box, where you can scroll through the options or do keywords search.

Up at the top of our dialog box, underneath the **OK** and **Cancel** buttons, there is a button for **Register to preset**. This will allow us to save the dimensions that we have just created and use them later on in other files. Click on the **Register to preset** button and then enter a descriptive name. We'll call our current settings Comic Strip—easy to remember and to the point.

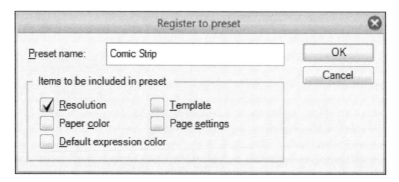

You can choose what options will be saved in your preset. **Resolution** is automatically checked. You can also save the template, if you are using one. This is handy if you are creating a strip, or something that usually has the same number and layout of panels. **Page settings** will save anything under the **Multiple pages** options, which is very handy if you have a comic that is always the same number of pages per chapter or storyline. And of course the **Default expression color** option can also be saved, so that your saved preset will always be whichever option you selected.

Now, click on **OK** in the dialog box and our **Comic Strip** template will be saved in to the **Preset** drop-down menu for us to use at any time.

At the bottom of our **New** dialog box are the **Multiple pages** options. This allows us to create many page files all at once and be able to organize them. The **Number of pages** dropdown gives some common number of pages, but you can also enter a custom number simply by clicking in the box and typing a number. The **Spread corresponding page(M)** option makes it possible to create two-page spreads with our files.

Binding point is the option for what side of the finished book the spine will be located on. I'm an English speaker, so I click on the **Left binding** option. If your book will be bound with the spine on the right, click on **Right binding**.

The **Start page** indicates which side the first page will be on. In books that are bound on the left, this is usually the right-hand page (because the back of the cover is usually blank, or filled with an advertisement in the case of mainstream comics publishing in the U.S.).

The **Save folder** is the folder on your hard drive where this file will be stored. The **Reference...** button beneath it allows you to change the folder by browsing your hard drive. Click on **Reference...** and choose where you want to store your file. Then the **Management folder** text is the new folder that Manga Studio will create to store the image files. This can be a storyline name, an issue number, anything that you desire, so long as you know what it is. Let's name our Management folder `Chapter One` for these exercises. The **Management file** text under the **Management folder** name changes as we change the folder name, to show us how our file is going to be set up on our hard drive.

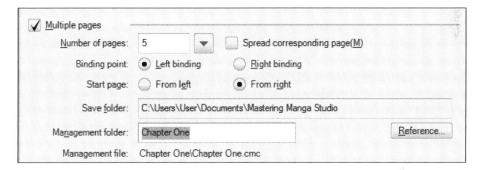

Now, click on the **OK** button to create your new file.

Navigating and rearranging pages

Once you click on **OK** and Manga Studio creates the pages, the **Page Manager** window will open. This window is the command center for our story file. We can see thumbnails of our pages, zoom in and out on them, and open pages to work on.

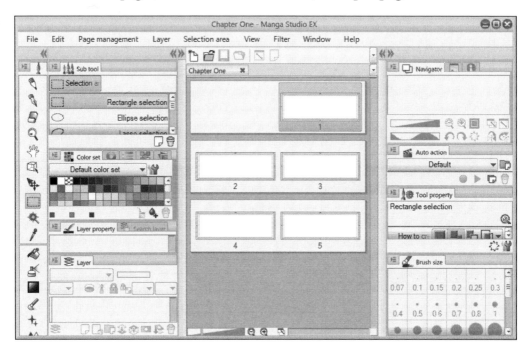

As you can see, in this view we can see thumbnails of all of our files in this story. This is great for a number of things, including being able to check the flow of your story. I often catch myself putting too many splash pages in a chapter of my comic, and I see that when I look over the pages in story mode. We can also rearrange pages in this tab.

To rearrange the pages, simply left-click on a page and drag-and-drop it in its new position. A red line will appear where the page will be dropped so that you can be sure you have it in the spot where you want it.

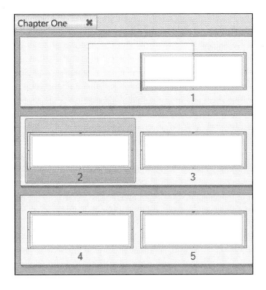

When you let go of the page in its new spot in the story, Manga Studio will need a moment to update all of the page information. Once that's done, you can continue working on your project.

At the bottom of your Manga Studio window, there are several options for zooming in and out of your page thumbnails. Three of these are the same options that are in your bottom toolbar when working on a canvas.

The first option is a slider that allows you to zoom in and out by dragging the light gray rectangle to the left or right. Click on it and drag to the right to zoom in. Dragging to the left will zoom back out on the thumbnails. If you're having trouble telling what pages in your story are what, you can zoom in to see them better, and then zoom out again to get a look at the visual flow of the entire chapter or a section of it all at once.

The next two icons in the lower bar are also for zooming in and out, but they do so by pre-set percentages. The right-most icon is the Fitting control, which can be toggled back and forth between the pages being laid out horizontally or vertically. Click on it and the pages will rearrange so that they're two across on the screen and fit inside the Manga Studio workspace.

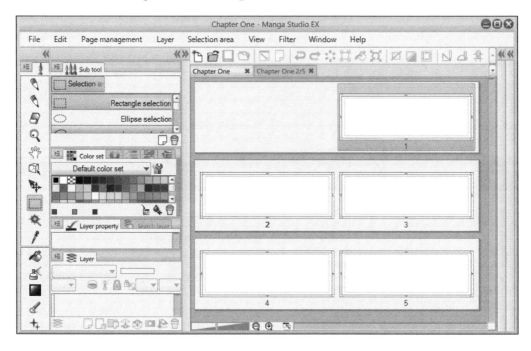

Alright, now you know how to zoom in and out of your page thumbnails, so we can explore some of the other things you can do in the story mode of Manga Studio.

The Story management menu

In the main menu bar of Manga Studio, click on the **Story** section and let's take a look at the options for navigating and changing our pages.

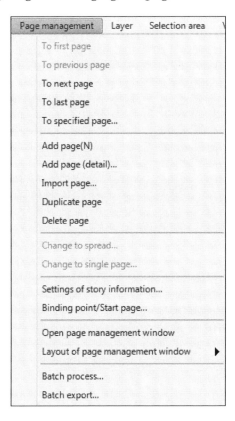

The first section of the menu options is incredibly useful if you're working on a longer comic project, say a full issue or a graphic novel. In our current project we have the first page selected, so the **To first page** and **To previous page** options are grayed out. On pages other than the first one, those options would be available, as would the other options in the menu that are not active on the first page.

As you can see, the first five options are for navigation. Say that you're on page 100 of your graphic novel and you need to go back to page 1, use the **To first page** option to get there quickly and without wasting time scrolling. You can also jump to the last page, to previous or next pages, or to a specific page. If you want to see page 32 of that 100 page story, just select the **To specified page...** option and enter the number of the page you want to jump to.

The second section of this menu allows us to add and otherwise change pages in our story. There are two options for adding pages. **Add page (N)** adds a page with the same settings as the pages already in the story file. **Add page (detail)...** will give us the same **New** options that we had when we made our comic strip template at the beginning of the chapter. Click on this now and add an A4-sized page from the drop-down menu to your story.

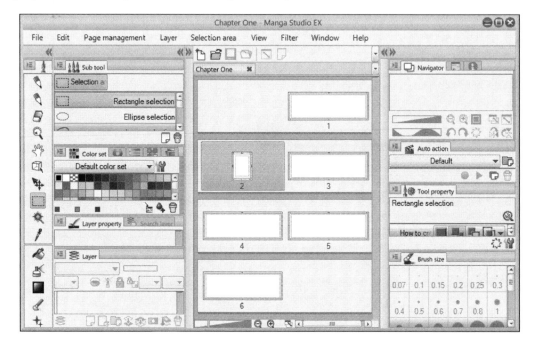

You can also use this as a shortcut to add more than one page to your file. Let's say that we wanted to take our file that now has 6 pages in it and make it 10 pages instead. Click on the **Add page (detail)...** option under Story Management. Make sure that the **Comic Strip** template is selected in the drop-down menu. Then, under the **Multiple pages** option, enter 4.

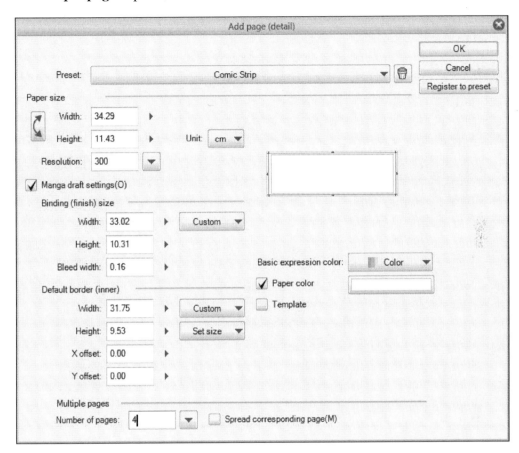

Click on **OK**, and Manga Studio adds four pages to the file, bringing our page count total to ten (one A4 size and nine Comic Strip size).

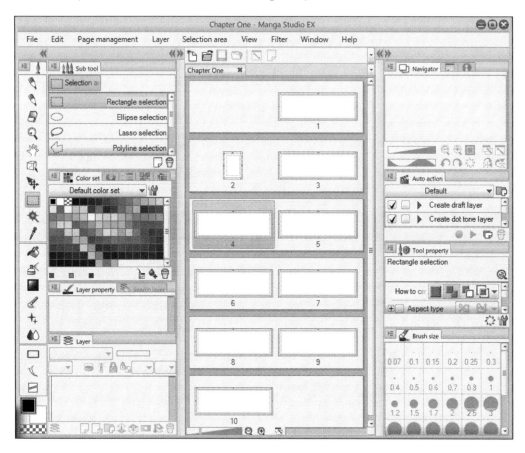

The next item in the menu is to import a page. Click on the **Import page...** option and navigate to a Manga Studio file, or an other graphic file on your computer and click on the **Open** button. **Import page** will bring the file in as a page on its own, so you can even take the previous images that you have drawn and compile them as individual pages, all in one file. Perhaps you need to include a previous scene in a chapter of your comic story as a flashback and you don't wish to redraw it. Import the pages and arrange them as needed and you're done!

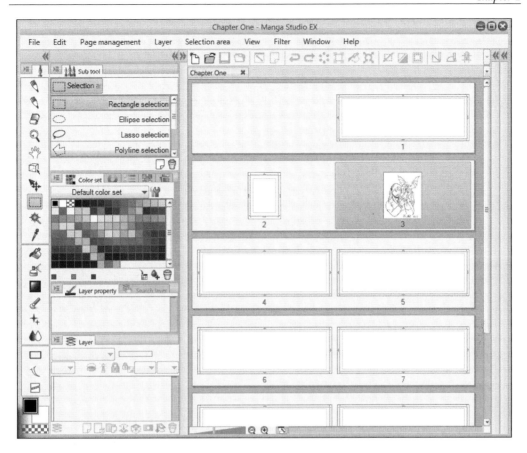

Let's say we want to duplicate page 2 of our file. Click on it so that it is highlighted with a blue box. Then go to the **Duplicate page** option under **Story** and select it. Now we have a copy of page 2, which is our A4-sized page.

Finally in this section we have the **Delete page** option. Stay on the copy of Page 2 and use **Delete page** to get rid of it. Manga Studio will show you the following warning:

You won't have to worry about deleting a page that you don't actually want gone. Since our copy of page 2 is empty, we'll go ahead and click on **OK**. Our file is now back down to 11 pages, one of which is an imported page with an image on it and the other ten are blank.

For the next two options under the **Story** menu, we'll need to select two facing pages that are both the same size and resolution. Each box that Manga Studio separates your pages in indicates that the pages contained are facing. Page 1 has no facing page because it's the first one, so it's in a box by itself. Click on page 4 in your file (it's facing with page 5 and they are both the **Comic Strip** template) and choose the **Change to spread** option.

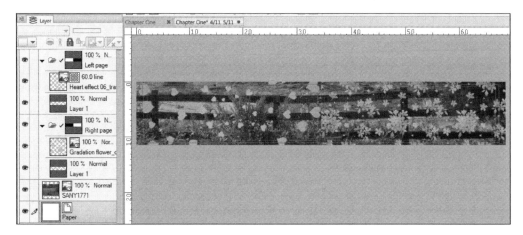

This combines the two pages together to form a two-page spread. Drawings and images can be added to both pages or to only the left or right page, as you can see in the previous screenshot.

The photo of the fence is on a layer beneath the folders for each side of the page, so it shows across them both. The pattern of the hearts is inside the left-page folder, so it only shows on the left side. The blue flowers, likewise, are in the right-page folder and so only show there.

Working on two-page spreads serves a few purposes. For one, two-page spreads can add drama to a comic. And for two, if you work in spreads you can save time by working on two pages at once instead of one at a time. This leads to less switching back and forth between pages, and therefore less wasted time, so you can draw more.

Don't want those pages to be joined in a spread anymore? Go back to the **Chapter One** tab so that you can see the page thumbnails. Then under Story Management, click on the **Change to single page...** menu item. A warning will appear as shown in the following screenshot:

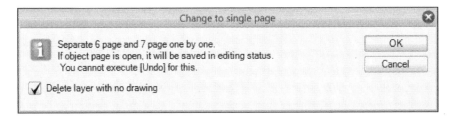

It's similar to the warning that we get when we join pages together into spreads, and is letting us know that this operation can't be reversed by clicking on the undo button. Click on **OK** though and take a look at the pages that were once a spread.

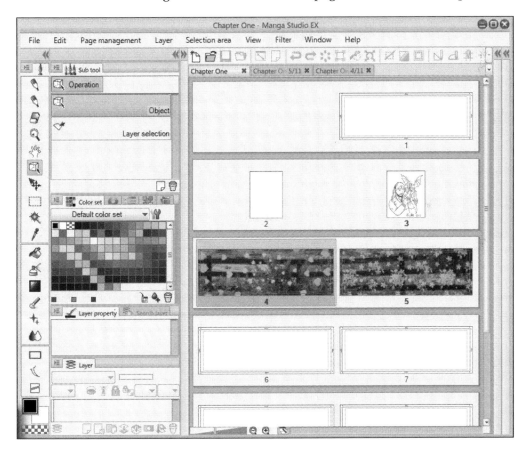

The pages have separated and none of the graphics on them have been lost. Let's say that we realized later that we didn't want these to be single pages after all. We could turn them back in to a spread again by using the **Change to spread...** command again and the pages will be combined.

There may be times when you will need to add page numbers, story names, or chapter information to the margins of your comic pages. This might be for publishing purposes or submission to a publisher. Whatever the reason may be, no need to put in that information by hand on each page, because Manga Studio can do it for you.

Go to the **Settings of story information...** option under the **Story** menu and click on it. This will bring up a dialog box that you can fill in with any story information that you need or want displayed on your pages.

Let's fill this in so you can see how it works. For the **Story name** field, let's put in `Mastering Manga Studio`. If you want to put in a number of stories, you can check the next box and put in a number using the menu to the right of the textbox. Text entered in to the **Subtitle** box will show up with the Story name. Let's enter `Chapter One` as the subtitle. Put your name in the **Author** box.

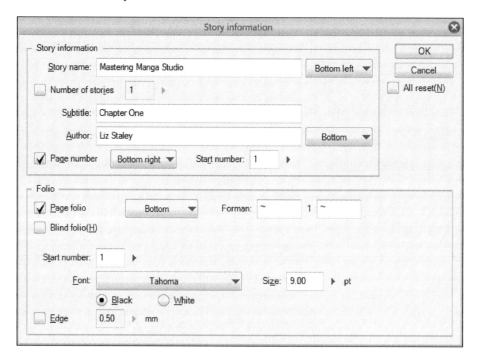

The **Page number** option will toggle page numbers on and off. You can also choose where the number will be displayed and what the start number for the story will be. This is very handy if you're producing an ongoing comic and wish to keep track of total page count instead of having every file start over at page one.

The **Folio** section of the **Story information** settings displays a page number just outside of the finished area, and inside of the bleed. The drop-down menu controls exactly where this is displayed, with options for the top and bottom of the page, and in the center, on the outside, or on the inside (which is the side of the page by the binding). If you want to add some other characters to the **Page folio** number, say on either side of the number, you can do so in the textboxes. Just to show how this works, let's put some ~ marks in either text box.

The **Blind folio** displays a page number in the inside of the page, near the binding.

Start number will change the starting number that is displayed, just like the **Start number** option in the **Story Information** section of this dialog box. Just below that are settings for the font and the size of the font, as well as the color. When you click on **OK**, something like the following screenshot should be displayed—it will differ according to what settings you have picked, but if you copied mine then it should look just like the following screenshot. Except with your name as the author, of course!

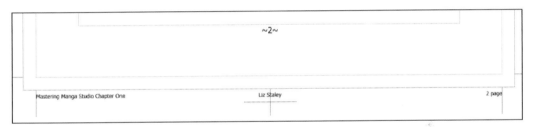

What if you accidentally set up your story file incorrectly and you set it for right binding instead of left? Not a problem because you can change it with the press of a button. One of the options in the **Story** menu is our **Binding point/Start page** option from the menu we created our file from in the beginning.

To change any of these settings, simply click on the radio button next to the correct option and click on **OK**.

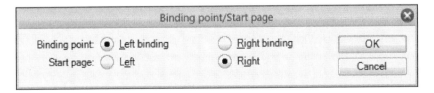

Until now, we've been working with the **Page Manager** window open and set as a tab (where you can view all of your pages as thumbnails and rearrange them). If you don't like this setup, Manga Studio allows you to customize where the window will display.

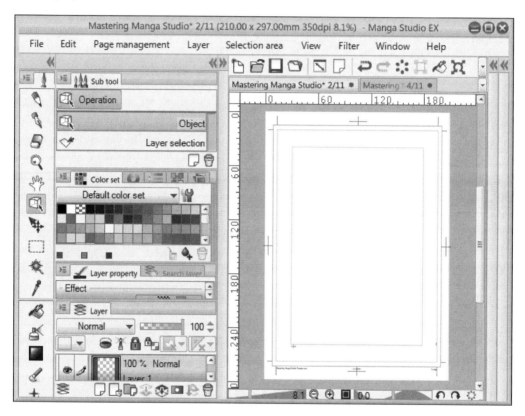

First, open one or two of your current pages by double-clicking on them so they show up in their own tabs. Then close the **Chapter One** tab by clicking on the black dot to the right of the tab name. Now you should only have a tab or two with active pages in them.

You can tell that these are pages within a story file because in their tabs, they have their page number and the total page count. The currently showing page in my file is number 2 of 11 pages. Now navigate to **Story | Page Manager Layout | Down**. Once you have done that, select the **Page Manager** option under the **Story** menu.

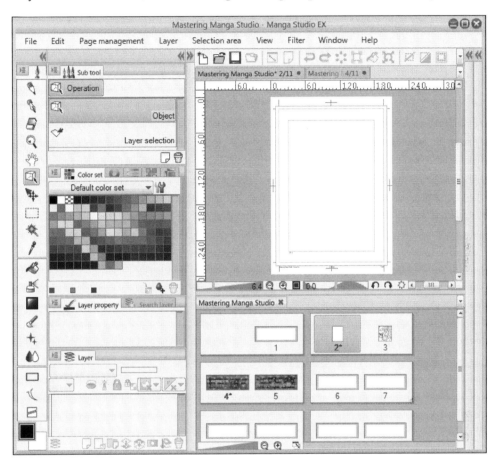

In order to change the page manager window again, you must close the current one and then open it again with the new settings in place. Close the currently open window, switch the layout to Right, and then open the window again with the menu commands. Now the page thumbnails will show on the right side of the screen.

The last two menu items that we're going to talk about for this chapter are the **Batch process** and **Batch export** options. Learn how to use these and you're going to save yourself a ton of time on your story projects.

Let's take a look at **Batch process** first. Navigate to **Story | Batch process** and the dialog box will be opened. **Batch process** allows us to perform something from the main menu or the auto actions (which we will cover in more detail in *Chapter 7, Ready! Set! Action!*) on any, some, or all of your pages. So let's say that we've drawn all of our pages and now we're ready to export them so we can put them on our website. If we drew them at a dpi of 300 or more because we're planning to print later, then the first thing we'll need to do is change the resolution of each page to 72 dpi.

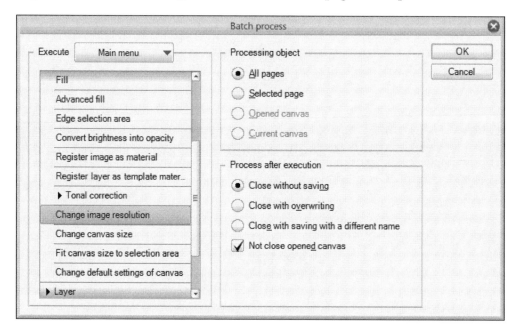

Using the arrows to the side of each menu option, you can expand and collapse each folder of operations. Under the **Main menu,** find and select **Change image resolution**. To the right of it, where we can pick what to execute, are several more settings. If we only wanted to apply this change to the currently highlighted page, we could choose that option. For right now we'll leave it as **All pages,** because we want all the pages in our story to have the resolution adjusted.

The second set of radio buttons is for what happens after the selected process is performed. The first option will close the opened page without saving (you will be prompted to save the page). The second will overwrite the existing file. The third will save the processed page with a different name and then close it.

The checkbox allows you to keep any opened pages open after the process has been completed.

Click on the **OK** button. A warning about the default border and crop marks being deleted may come up. Tell Manga Studio to proceed with the operation.

Now the program will open page 1 of our file and show the following window. Set **Resolution** to **72**.

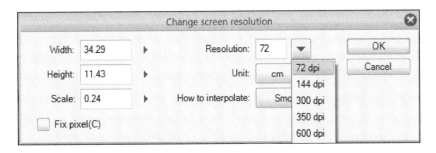

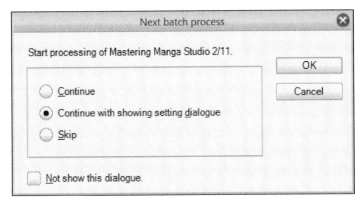

Now click on **OK** again. Because we left the **Close without saving** option in the **Batch process** window on, we will be asked if we want to save the current page before it's closed. Click on the **Save** button.

Now the program moves on to the next page. We can continue using the same settings that we used on page 1, or we can continue and see the setting dialog box again to select a different resolution setting. We can also skip the second page if we don't wish to process it at this time.

Checking the **Not show this dialogue** checkbox will finish the process without showing the previous box. If you chose to continue without seeing the setting dialog, then the process will continue, making each page into a 72 dpi file and then prompting if you'd like to save it or not.

Once that's complete, you can then batch export your files into a different format.

Navigate to **Story | Batch export**.

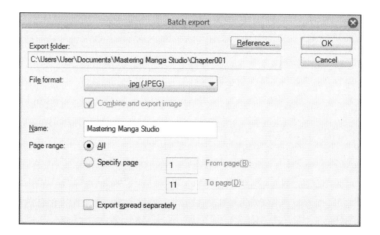

Use the **Reference...** button to browse to the folder where you want to store your exported images. Then select a file format from the drop-down menu. You can change the name of the files, and specify whether or not to export all the pages or just a range of pages. Click on **OK**. In the next window you will be asked to adjust your JPG settings. Set them how you like and then click on **OK** again.

Now if we go to the folder we specified in the **Export folder** box, we'll see that we have a JPG file for each of the 11 pages that we created in our story.

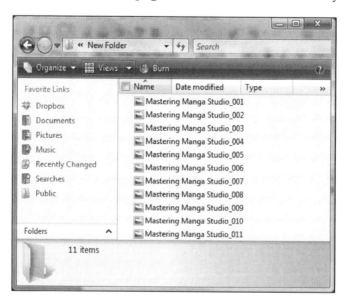

Summary

Now you know all that you need to about how to use the Story features of Manga Studio! You're ready to create your comics, sketchbooks, art books, or any other sort of books, because we have learnt about the following topics:

- Creating a new story file
- Making custom page templates and saving them
- Reorganizing pages
- Adding, deleting, importing, and duplicating pages
- Editing story info and page numbers
- Changing the layout of the Page Manager window
- Batch processing and exporting

Now we're ready to get to some drawing. And to do that, we're going to want to know how to make our own tools to further customize Manga Studio and make it our own. That's just what we're going to be doing in the next chapter, so let's get to work!

The Right Tools for the Job
2

In this chapter we're going to explore the different drawing and painting tools in Manga Studio and make custom ones. Many Manga Studio 5 users are sharing their custom brushes on the web right now, and after completing this chapter you'll be able to share your tools with them.

This chapter will cover:

- Benefits of making your own tools
- How to make a pencil tool
- Making an inking brush
- Creating a paintbrush that mimics the traditional medium
- Explanations of the custom drawing tool options
- Importing and exporting your tools

The benefits of using custom tools

Manga Studio 5 comes equipped with some great tools, pencils, pens, India ink, watercolor, and oil brushes, just to name a few. But knowing how to make custom tools can help speed your process along, especially if you find yourself doing repetitive tasks that could be left to a custom brush instead. An example of this is putting leaf texture on a tree. Instead of doing this by hand, you could customize a brush to create the effect for you. A few tweaks, a custom texture, and your tedious task just became a whole lot easier.

You can also create custom tools to mimic a huge number of traditional art mediums. If you like to sketch with a non-photo blue mechanical pencil, then do your drawing with charcoal pencil, and finally paint over the whole thing with acrylic paints. All of those steps can be mimicked using Manga Studio's coloring engine. It takes some patience, and some tweaking, to make your own tools. But once you get the hang of it, and get a library of custom tools made, you'll be flying through making your illustrations and comic pages.

And now that it's easy to import and export the tools that you've made, the possibilities are endless. You can share your settings, or even sell your tools as downloadable content to other Manga Studio users through your site. Pretty cool, huh? Let's get started and make some custom tools to play around with!

Making a custom pencil tool

In the following section we're going to make a pencil tool to use for sketching. It will give you a traditional pencil look, just like the following screenshot:

In order to make any custom tool, the process to start is going to be the same. Since we're going to create a pencil in this exercise, click on the pencil tool in your Manga Studio toolbox (so that when we're done, our custom pencil will show up as a sub tool for us here, rather than being somewhere else, like the inking or painting tools). At the top of your tools menu is the icon to open the **Sub tool** menu, to which the arrow in the following screenshot points:

Click on it and then select **Create custom sub tool** from the menu.

The following dialog box will come up:

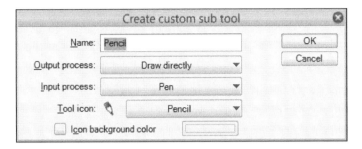

Enter a **Name** text for your new tool. In this case we'll go with `Sketching Pencil`. The **Output process** dropdown tells Manga Studio what you want this tool to do. For most of these, we'll be using **Draw directly**, because we want to make marks on a layer with the tools that we're creating. One of the great things about Manga Studio 5 though is that you can make custom tools for any of their sub tools, including custom Zoom tools and Eyedropper tools.

The **Tool icon** dropdown is where you can select what shows up in your toolbox when you have your new sub tool selected. Below that is the checkbox where you can set the **Icon background color** if you wish to use a custom color behind the default icon.

Color code your icon backgrounds! It will make your custom tools easier to find, and tell you exactly what tool you have active when you're switching between tools in your toolbox bar.

Let's go ahead and set a custom color for this tool's icon background. Check the checkbox next to the **Icon background color** text to activate the option. Then click on the box to the right that will be filled with black once you turn the option on. Since we're making a sketching pencil, and I usually associate sketching with the non-photo blue pencils, let's choose a blue color. Clicking on **OK** will then bring up the **Sub tool detail** screen. This is where the fun starts, though all of the options can look overwhelming at first! But really, once you know the basics of what each option does, it's fun to play around with them. If you'd rather explore these options yourself but would like a rundown of what each one does, check out the end of this chapter for descriptions and examples of the different effects. If you want to do some guided exercises before striking out and going crazy with your custom tools, stay with me.

First up we'll visit the **Brush size** menu. I like my sketching lines to be fairly thin, so we'll start off with a 4.0 setting.

 You can change the size of your brush on the fly by using the keyboard shortcuts [and], to make them smaller and larger, respectively.

The next effect that I want for my pencil is to make it layered like a real pencil. You know when you draw with a regular pencil, how the lead gets darker if you go over an area many times? A way to get that same look from our digital pencil tool is to go under the **Ink** menu. I'd rather not change the **Opacity** value from **100** percent on my pencil, so instead we'll just set the **Combine mode** dropdown to **Multiply**.

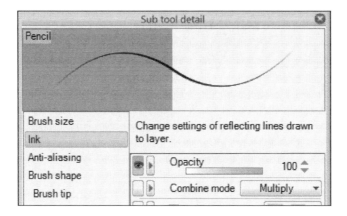

I know what you're thinking. Why not change the **Opacity** value down to about 50 percent? You'd get the same layering effect from the Sketching Pencil that way, because as you put 50 percent opacity lines down over one another, they would build up in density and become darker. However, it's a different look than using a Multiply Combine Mode, and the lines start off much lighter than I like when I'm sketching, especially if I'm sketching a layout in a light color. So that's why I choose to change **Combine mode** instead of **Opacity**, at least for this particular tool that we're making.

So right now we've got a pretty good looking tool. We could use it and it would function well. But we could make it look and act even more like a pencil.

For that the next option that we're going to look at is the **Brush tip** option, which is indented under the **Brush shape** option in our dialog box. Here we have several options, one of the most important ones being the **Tip shape** option at the top. Here you can set the brush to either be a circular tip or a tip based on a material (or materials, because you can use more than one) from the materials library.

Let me provide a quick word on materials now. Materials are a lot of things, but for the purpose of making our custom tools, materials are symbols or textures. There are many of these loaded into Manga Studio already, including splatters, cross hatching, and even items such as lace and patterns. We can use these symbols or textures to modify the way that the brush operates and get special effects, like traditional pencil or the look of a rough brush.

Okay, back to our brush tip! Clicking on the **Material** option will activate the rectangle beneath, where we can select our materials to apply to this brush. Click in the rectangle which says **Click here and add tip shape** and a dialog box of available materials is shown. If you know what keywords have been applied to the material you want, you can search for it on the left. Or just scroll down until you find something that you like.

For our sketching tool let's select the **Blurred spray** material. Click on it to highlight it and then click on **OK** to have it applied. You'll be able to see a preview of what your pencil tool will look like in use in the **Sub tool detail** screen.

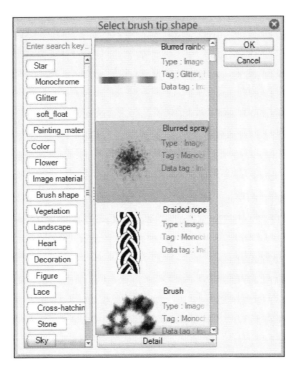

Next we're going to play with the thickness and the direction of the `Sketching Pencil`. Underneath the **Tip shape** option (where we just selected our material) we have several sliders. The first one that we're going to adjust is the **Thickness** slider. This slider controls the width of the brush tip in either the horizontal or vertical direction, depending on which option you have selected. Switch to the vertical option and take the slider down to **60**. This will give us an oval shaped brush tip that will give a bit of irregularity to our pencil marks.

Leaving the rest of the options on this menu as they are will give us a serviceable pencil tool, and you could stop here if you're happy with the results that you're getting so far. I personally don't like the straight flat tip of the current settings. Luckily the **Direction** slider will allow us to change the rotation of the tip so that we get a broader line. This one I've set to **100.0** so that it's slightly angled. The slider is set from 0 to 360, with 0 being no rotation, and 360 being a full rotation. Setting it to **100.0** gets us a slightly angled oval that will work nicely for some pencil lines.

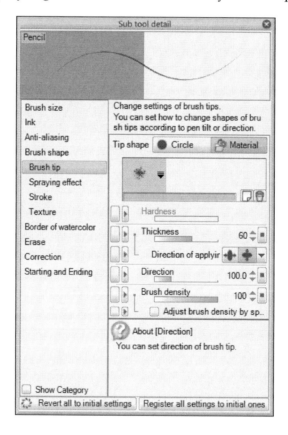

The last thing we should think about doing is setting a texture option to make our lines a bit rougher and have some more character to them. To do that, let's head down to the **Texture** menu. The way that this reacts on the brush strokes is a little different than the **Materials** option under the **Brush tip** menu. **Texture** acts more like a paper texture than anything (at least, if you ask me it does), so you can get the effect of drawing on different surfaces with your custom tool.

Clicking on the rectangle next to **Texture** (which, by default, will say **None**) will bring up our available options for textures to apply. As you can see, there are lots of options to play with. For this pencil tool though let's take the **Canvas** option, near the top of the list. The rest of the options under texture allow us to adjust how the texture we've selected will affect the marks we put down with our new pencil.

Reverse density makes the white pixels of the texture black and the black pixels white. **Emphasize density** will make the texture stronger and more noticeable. For this particular brush, I've turned both of those options on because I like the look that it's giving for these pencils. Take a look at the following screenshot:

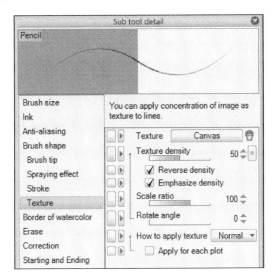

And with that, our `Sketching Pencil` is all done! You can close the **Sub tool detail** box and begin sketching with your new tool.

Made a bunch of changes that just aren't working? Want to go back to the settings that you started building your tool with? Click on the **Revert all to initial settings** button at the bottom of the **Sub tool detail** screen.

Your new pencil will show up as a tool under the **Pencil** sub tool menu. If you want to do any further editing (because you used the new pencil and realized you don't like the look of it after all, maybe), simply click on the show sub tool detail palette at the bottom of the **Tool property** palette. It looks like a little wrench and will pull the menus back up for you to edit to your heart's content.

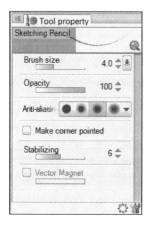

Making a custom inking pen

Manga Studio has excellent inking tools right out of the box (so to speak!). The default tools under the pen mimic several standard inking tools very well, including the very popular G pen which is a standard for many manga artists. It also has a calligraphy and a mapping pen, any of which might fit your style of inking very well. But let's say that we want a pen tool that reacts more like an inking brush instead of a pen. So we'll want to make a custom tool that has a bit more to give and maybe a bit more texture to the edges, so that we get the look of inking with bristles. Plus we'll want a lot of flexibility between the thick and the thin strokes.

So let's get started, and we'll make a brush that will give us this effect over our sketch that we did with our pencil tool.

Select the **Ink** tool in your toolbox, since that's where we're going to want this tool to show up when we're finished with it. When you click on the **Ink** option, the sub tool palette will change to show you the already available options. Click on the icon at the top of the **Sub tool palette** option and click on the **Create custom sub tool** button from the options under the menu.

We're going to call this one Brush Ink, since I want to attempt to recreate something close to the Pentel pocket brush that I love the most for doing traditional inking. This is a drawing tool, so we're going to leave it as **Draw directly** in the **Output process** dropdown and **Pen** in the **Input process** dropdown. Let's give it an icon background color. I'm going to choose a nice green, but you can choose whatever color you like that will make it easy for you to remember what this tool is when it's showing in your toolbox.

Once we have that done we're going to click on **OK** and we'll be taken back to the **Sub tool detail** menu that we saw in the last exercise.

Let's start off with the **Brush size** option. We're trying to emulate a bristle brush here, so something very important is going to be that that tool transitions from thin lines to thick ones as we press more on our tablet pen. That way it will mimic the pressure that you could put on a real brush. First of all let's set our initial brush size to about **20.0**. This gives the option for some really nice, thick lines, but we can also set it to do things as well depending on the pen pressure.

To the right of the **Brush size** option is a downward facing arrow. Click on it and another menu will appear that will let us set the brush size to react to different factors. The checkboxes next to these options turn them on and off. **Tilt** manages the brush size according to the amount of tilt that your tablet pen has while making your stroke. **Velocity** relies on how quickly you move your table stylus. **Random** gets you a random bunch of line widths when you make a brush stroke.

These options can be layered one on top of the other to create more unique effects. Turn on both **Pen pressure** and **Random** at the same time to see the stroke preview and you'll understand what I mean. This, combined with the plethora of other options when creating custom tools, can give you endless style options for your art.

Alright, so we'll check the box next to the **Pen pressure** checkbox to turn it on. Then we set the **Min value** slider to about **2**, as that will give us thin lines when we use light pressure, but with the brush size being set at **20.0** we have the option for lovely thick lines as well, and transitioning between the two.

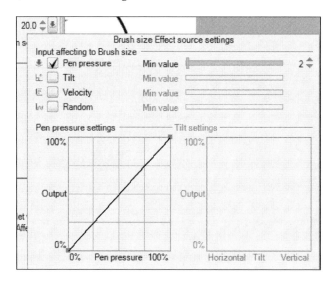

Now we need to make this brush have a bit of texture so that we get the brush bristle effect. We don't want anything too overt, just more of a variation than the perfectly circular-brush shape we have right now. Head down to the **Brush tip** option and click on the box marked **Material**. You're going to click in the rectangle below that now that says **Click here and add tip shape**. This will bring up your **Material** options.

Let's navigate down the **Material** menu until we find **Droplet 1**—or you can simply type Droplet into the search bar at the top left of the **Materials** window, and the material that we want will come right up. Left-click to highlight it and then click on **OK**.

This material as is doesn't do a whole lot to the look of our stroke. However, by changing the direction of the brush tip, we can get some variation in how the tool reacts. Pull the slider under **Direction** to the right and keep your eye on the brush stroke preview in the top of the **Sub tool detail** menu. It will update in real time to show you a preview of what your finished brush would look like. As you can see, some direction values produce a thinner overall line, while some are thicker. I settled on **225.0** as my direction because I like that it has a little variation in the center of the stroke, still keeping the option for the thick lines.

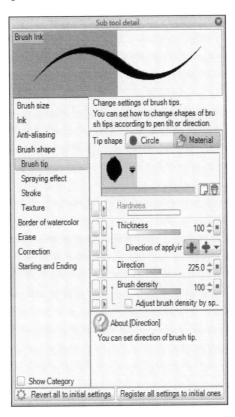

In order to break up the brush a little more and give us a bit more texture on the edges, go to the **Stroke** menu and click on the **Wide** option. By default the new tool should start out on **Normal**, and **Wide** is one box to the left. Then, under the **Correction** options we're going to check the box next to the **Correct by speed** option.

Finally we're going to go to the **Starting and Ending** settings and make one quick change. Clicking in the drop-down menu by the **Starting and Ending** option in this menu brings up a menu similar to the one that we used earlier in the **Brush size** options, where we can set different options to be effected and the minimum value for each. Turn on the **Brush size** option in the **Starting and Ending** drop-down and set the minimum value to **3**. **Starting** and **Ending** can both stay set to **20**, the **Methods** dropdown can stay at **By length**, and the **Starting and Ending by speed** checkbox should be checked.

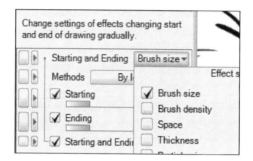

Close the **Sub tool detail** menu, and now your new ink brush is ready to take on some pencils!

Want to be able to change a setting for a tool without having to open the **Sub tool detail** menu every time? Checking the box to the left of the option you want to adjust will make it show up in the **Tool property** menu when you have your tool selected! Make sure that the box has a picture of an eye in it and the option will appear.

Paint away with a custom paintbrush

So now that we've made a pencil to draw with, and an inking brush to ink with, it's time to get into some coloring. Or rather, some painting. I have to admit to the fact that I have a slight obsession with speed painting brushes. (If you've never seen speed paintings, you should go and look some up on the Internet right now. And if you're feeling adventurous, try a few! They're great warm-up exercises!) Let's make a brush inspired by a speed painting brush. It's going to give us lovely, soft texture that mimics traditional brush strokes. Take a look at the colored picture below, which was digitally painted entirely with the brush we're about to make. Even the linework, which was inked with the inking brush that we just made, had the transparency locked and was gone over in more subtle, softer colors with it!

Before we can start painting with our custom brush, we're going to make a custom material to use as our brush tip. To do this, you'll need a blank canvas, any size. You can do this on a new page or use one of the pages in the Story file that we've already set up, whichever works best for you.

Click on the paintbrush tool in Manga Studio and then click on the **Watercolor** group in the **Sub tool** menu. Click on the **Transparent watercolor** brush and a medium gray shade, and then paint a soft-sided, uneven triangle with it. I like using the transparent watercolor and a medium gray because it gives some variation in the shading of the material we're making. Your triangle doesn't have to be exactly like the one in the example below, just try to keep the corners round and put a little variation in the shading.

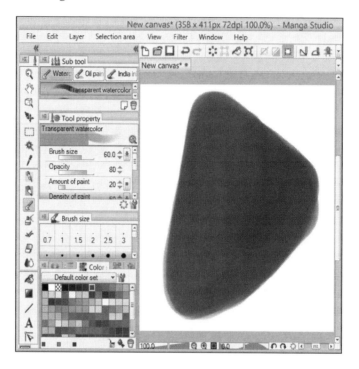

We have to register the triangle that we just painted as a **Material** now. This is done simply by going to the **Edit** menu at the top of the Manga Studio window and choosing the **Register image as Material** option.

Let's enter `Soft Triangle` as the **Material name** here, and make sure that the **Use for brush tip shape** checkbox is checked under our **Material image** preview. You can elect to save your material in whatever category on the right side of the **Material property** menu you wish. I chose **Monochromic pattern** because this is monochromatic, so it made sense to me. Another logical choice would be the **Image material** folder.

Once you have that filled in, click on the **OK** button and Manga Studio will save your new brush tip material. Now we are ready to make our brush! You should already be in the paintbrush tool because we used the watercolor option to make our material, but if you're not, then please select the paintbrush in your toolbox now. Then click on the **Oil paint** group in the **Sub tool** category.

The most important thing to remember about what **Sub tool** menu to put your custom tools in is where will you remember that it's stored? I chose the **Oil paint** group for this tool because that's what it most resembles when finished. But if putting it in the **Watercolor** or **India ink** group is better for you because you'll be able to find your brush easier, then by all means go for it!

Click on the icon in the upper left of the **Sub tool** palette and choose the **Create custom sub tool** option. Let's name this tool `Texture Brush` for now. Our **Output process** dropdown is going to be **Draw directly**, as with the tools we've previously made. I chose an orange color for my icon background.

Clicking on **OK** will take us to the **Sub tool detail** screen, where we can tweak our brush settings to our heart's content. The first thing we're going to want to do is go apply our brush material, so we can see if this is going to give the effect that we're looking for.

Click on **Brush tip**, and then the box for **Material**. Click to add brush tip, and that will bring up our list of materials that are available to use as a brush tip. Our Soft Triangle material should be at the top of the list, so left-click on it and then click on **OK**. Under the same menu, click on the downward arrow next to **Thickness** and turn on the **Pen pressure** option. This is going to make it such that the harder we press with our stylus, the thicker the pen tip is, and the lighter we press, the thinner it will be. In the following screenshot you can see the difference in the strokes made with the **Pen pressure** option turned off (top) and with it turned on (bottom). Note how the bottom line tapers off on the ends while the top does not!

 When making custom brushes, be sure to have a blank canvas active. You can adjust your settings and then test them out to tweak them just by clicking off the **Sub tool detail** screen and drawing on the canvas. This is much easier than closing the window and opening it back up again any time you want to test your brush!

Next up we need to make some adjustments under the **Ink** option in the **Sub tool detail** screen. It's the second menu option on the left-hand side, so click there and let's take a look at the options here.

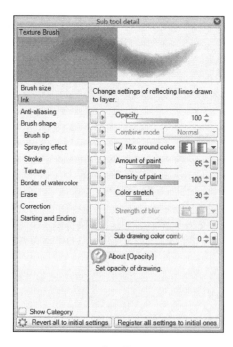

Leave the **Opacity** at **100**, and be sure that the **Mix ground color** checkbox is checked. The **Mix ground color** option will take colors that have already been put down on the layer that is active in Manga Studio, and mix them with a new color that's being put down by the brush tool. This allows for a soft transition between colors that will give a painted effect. The sliders beneath the **Mix ground color** option allow us to adjust how much paint is applied, the thickness of that paint, and how far the base color will be stretched into the new color. Feel free to adjust these options to suit your preferences, but the image above shows what I settled on.

That's just how easy it is to make a really unique brush that will give us a soft, hand-painted look in Manga Studio! Try out making different materials and using them as brushes. I usually get my inspiration by looking at the application resources on DeviantArt.com to see the effects that others have gotten, and then try to adjust them to my own personal taste and style. Remember that your art should be a reflection of you, so don't be afraid to experiment with your tools and make them work the way you like!

The following screenshot is an example of the color mixing and the look that can be achieved with the brush that we just made. The top three lines of color were made by laying down a base color and then picking another to go over top of it, blending the two together. The fourth is a gradient scale made with black, shades of gray, and white. The bottom line was done by putting down white with the brush first, and then blending light blue and purple into it.

Make a custom text tool

First we'll select the text tool (T), and then navigate to the **Create custom sub tool** setting under the **Sub tool** menu.

Clicking on this will open a menu that allows us to pick a few initial settings for our sub tool. Pick a name for your tool—maybe the name of the comic that you're going to be using this style of lettering on. I'm choosing the name Strange Text because of a character named Steven Strange that I will introduce you to later on in the book. Next click on **OK** and we'll be taken to the **Sub tool detail** screen. Here we can set our font face, size, and if we want to, we can use bold or underline styles on the **Font** tab.

For this tool, I'm going to use **Arial Black** as the **Font** and set it to **12.0** points.

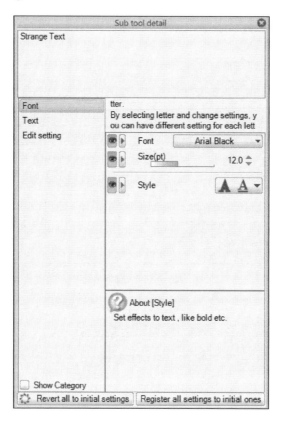

Clicking on the **Text** option to the left of this menu allows us to set **Justification** and **Line spacing**. Let's set our font tool to **Center** justification, so that our text lines for dialog will be centered to one another.

The **Edit setting** menu allows you to change the direction of the text from horizontal to vertical. It also has a setting for the display quality while editing text. If you find that, while working with text, you are clicking the corner handles a lot and accidentally resizing when you didn't want to, you can even turn off having the ability to resize text that way right in the **Edit setting** menu.

When you're done adjusting your text settings, you can just click on the cross in the upper right of the **Sub tool detail** screen. Your changes are automatically saved.

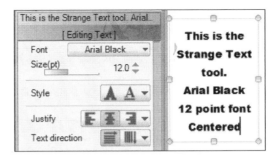

Now any time that we want to use text with this combination of settings, all we have to do is select the **Strange Text** custom tool from the **Text** sub tool menu. And the great thing is that we still have access to being able to change the text size, font, or style without having to change the tool settings too.

Now that you know the basics of making your own tools, go out there and experiment! The next section breaks down all the options available under the **Sub tool detail** menu, for easy reference while you're making your custom tools.

The custom sub tool options explained

The following section can be used as reference for all of the custom brush tool options available when making a pencil, pen, or paint brush.

Brush size menu

The **Brush size** menu options in the **Sub tool detail** dialog box.

Brush size

Change the initial size of the tool. The greater the number of the brush size, the larger the brush. You can always change the size while you're working with the brush, but this will set the initial size.

Specify by size on screen

This keeps the brush tip the same size in proportion to the zoom of your working canvas. Turn this on if you zoom in and out of your canvas a lot and don't want to change your brush size all the time. While you're zoomed in closer to the canvas, lines will appear thinner. Zoom further out and they will appear thicker. The following screenshot is a 72 dpi canvas with a 15.0 pixel brush. The top line was drawn at 100 percent, the middle was drawn at 200 percent, and the bottom was at 400 percent. When zoomed out, the lines appear thinner or thicker depending on the zoom on the canvas.

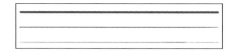

Atleast 1 pixel

This makes sure that a line of at least 1 pixel is being produced, no matter how light the pressure that is used on your tablet surface.

Ink menu

The **Ink** menu options in the **Sub tool detail** dialog box.

Opacity

How transparent the brush stroke is. 100 percent opacity will give the currently selected color at full strength. 50 percent is half strength. The following screenshot has black lines at 100 percent, 50 percent, and 20 percent opacity.

Combine mode

How the strokes interact with strokes that are already laid down. How these react to one another will depend on the colors that you're using, but in the following screenshot I used blue for the base strokes and then red to go over them. Look at the difference in the look of the red with each **Combine mode**.

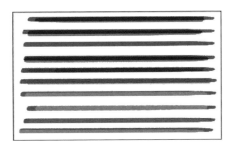

The combine modes used on the red color are **Darken**, **Multiply**, **Color Burn**, **Lineal Burn**, **Black Burn**, **Subtract**, **Lighten**, **Screen**, **White Burn**, and **Add**. It takes some experimenting to get the effect that you want with **Combine mode**.

Mix ground color

Great for getting painted effects, this option mixes the color of the current brush with any color already laid down on the canvas. This is sort of painting with wet oils. There are following options under the **Mix ground color** menu that adjust how Manga Studio does this:

- **Amount of paint**: This is the percentage of the already applied color with the new color. The larger the number, the more of the new drawing color will be mixed with the previous color.

- **Density of paint**: It shows how much of the new color is applied at the start of the stroke. The higher this number, the more severe the blend will be. A lower number results in a more gradual blend.

- **Strength of blur**: This is the amount of blur applied to the surrounding colors. The **Auto setting** option for this will use a blur amount based on the size of your brush. Turning it to fixed allows you to manually adjust this option for more or less blur.

- **Sub drawing color combined**: This is the strength of the underlying, already applied color. The smaller this number, the more of the new color there will be in the stroke. If the number is larger, then there will be more of the previous color instead.

Anti-aliasing menu

This is the setting for how the edges of your strokes are rendered. Perhaps you have zoomed in on a line in a graphics program before and seen a jagged edge with the pixels, rather than the edge being smooth. These options allow you to make the edge of the stroke with your custom tool harder or softer, depending on your preference. As you can see in the following screenshot, the top line was created with no anti-aliasing, while the bottom was drawn with strong anti-aliasing. Note that there are no more stray pixels coming off the edge of the line.

Brush shape menu

This changes the brush tip to a pre-set condition. For example, if you were making a custom pen and liked the pre-set pen tool, you could choose that and click on "Apply" and then edit from there. You can also save your current brush shape settings as a pre-set so that you can then apply it to other sub tools in the future.

Brush tip

This menu allows you to modify the tip of the brush. You can set the tip to either be a plain circle, or to use a pattern from your registered materials. We're going to talk about materials in-depth in *Chapter 5, Living in a Material World*, including how to make custom ones. Selecting a material to base your brush shape on allows you to get cool effects, such as clouds, flower petals, or other textures. The options in this menu are as follows:

- **Hardness**: This option controls how sharp the edges of the brush are. The larger the number, the harder the edge will be. If you're making a brush that you want to blend in softly with the rest of the image, set this to a low number.

- **Thickness**: Your new tool's overall dimension can be controlled with this slider. This option has a horizontal or vertical control located under the slider bar. In traditional media terms, using this option on a circular brush tip would turn it into an oval (or flat) brush.

- **Direction**: This is the rotation of the brush tip. 0 is no rotation. 180 is half a rotation, and 360 is a full rotation. This will seem to have no effect on a perfectly circular brush. The following screenshot was created with a 60 thickness round brush. The second line is set at zero rotation, so that you can see how it looks like a perfectly circular brush even though it's really an oval. The other lines are various amounts of rotation on the same brush thickness.

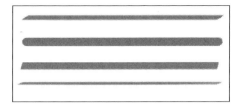

- **Brush density**: This option shows how heavy the brush stroke is on the canvas. A larger number will give you a darker brush. A smaller number will give you a less dense, and therefore lighter, stroke.

 If you change settings in **Brush tip** and then change anything under the **Brush shape** option, your **Brush tip** will be reset!

Spraying effect

When this option is turned on using the checkbox next to the **Spraying effect** option, the brush will produce a spray paint look.

- **Particle size**: This option shows how large the individual paint particles are. A smaller number produces a finer spray, while a larger number gives a thicker "blobby" spray.
- **Particle density**: This shows how close together the individual particles are.
- **Spray deviation**: This option controls the width of the spray. A lower, negative number produces a wider spray. A positive, larger number produces a thinner spray.

- **Deviation of particle**: This sets the angle of the brush tip.

Stroke

The various options to configure the stroke are as follows:

- **Space**: This option sets the spacing of the brush tips closer together. Making the spacing larger will produce polka dot or uneven lines, while setting them closer together will produce a smoother one.

- **Continuous spraying**: This makes the stroke continuous, so that it keeps applying color whether the cursor is moving or not. This can produce a "blob" at the end of some strokes that will make them look even more like spray paint.

- **Ribbon**: This option is used to make effect brushes like the zigzag, music notes, and lace brushes that come with Manga Studio 5. (These can be found under the **Decoration brush** menu.) Turning this option on will take multiple brush materials applied to a brush and repeat it as a ribbon, like rolling out a piece of lace or a tape.

- **Repeat type**: This shows how the pattern is repeated for the **Ribbon** mode. The following screenshot shows a brush made with three tip materials. The first row is the **Repeat** option. The second row is the **Reverse** option. The third row shows the **No repeat** option, which simply uses the first two materials and then the last material for the rest of the stroke. The final row is the **Random** option, which will produce a random spread of the materials.

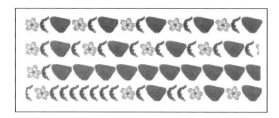

- **Blend brush tips by darken**: Turning this on will take the overlapping shapes (determined by the spacing!) and darken them as you use your custom tool.

Texture

This menu allows you to apply a texture to your strokes. It's different from the **Material** option under the **Brush tip** menu because this acts more like a paper texture than anything. This menu has following options:

- **Texture**: This allows selecting a texture to apply to the stroke. There are many different options in Manga Studio 5, including canvas and brick.

- **Density**: This is the amount of the texture that's applied to the stroke. The less dense, the less obvious this texture will be.

- **Reverse density**: This option will reverse the black and white pixels of the texture.

- **Emphasize density**: This makes the texture stronger and more noticeable. Great for special effect brushes like charcoal or brick walls.

- **Scale ratio**: This is the size of the applied texture.

- **Rotate angle**: This is the angle of the texture as it's applied to the stroke.

- **How to apply texture**: This is a selection of blending modes specific to the texture. **Normal, Multiply, Subtract, Compare,** and **Outline**. Each one changes how the texture is blended to the tool stroke. You can adjust these settings and see a preview of how the changes will take in the stroke preview at the top of the window.

- **Apply for each plot**: This option controls how Manga Studio renders the texture for each time that you make a mark with your custom tool. Leaving this unchecked will treat the texture as though it were lying on the paper, so each stroke will "reveal" some of the texture, and it will repeat based on the scale ratio setting you have used. Checking this box will have the program layer the texture with each mark made with the brush, so that you will get a more random, layered effect. Note the repeat of the texture in the first set of strokes in the following example; this was made using the canvas texture and not applying for each plot. The bottom set of marks was made with the same settings, but having Manga Studio apply the texture to each stroke.

Border of watercolor menu

This menu will allow you to get a watercolor effect with your new brush by adding an edge around the stroke. The included options in this menu are as follows:

- **Border of watercolor**: This option turns the watercolor option on and off with the checkbox. The slider makes the border more or less noticeable.

- **Opacity impact**: This shows how solid the outer line is.

- **Brightness impact**: This affects how dark or light the outer line is. The following screenshot shows first a brush stroke with the default **Border of watercolor** settings. The second line has the **Opacity impact** option turned to **100**. The third one has both **Opacity** and **Brightness** set to **100**. Note how much darker the outside border is for each of these.

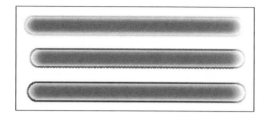

- **Process after drag**: This little checkbox is a must-check if you are working on a machine with a limited amount of RAM. Turning this on will process the watercolor edge after you've made the line with your brush, rather than rendering it while drawing. This can save you a lot of memory on your machine and up the performance if you need it.

Erase menu

This menu is only active if you are making a new eraser. If you are working with a vector layer, you can make an eraser that erases vectors in different ways, including only erasing the sections that you indicate, erasing the vector up to an intersection with another vector, or erasing the entire vector line with one click.

The second option under this menu is to make an eraser that erases on all layers, no matter which layer you have selected as your active layer.

Correction menu

This menu controls the amount and types of correction that are automatically available for the program to handle for you while you are drawing. If you have shaky hands, these options are pretty invaluable actually. They can also be handy if you work on lots of cityscapes or mechanical objects because you can set the correction to smooth your lines as you work and it will save you time. The options are follows:

- **Make corner pointed**: Turning this option on will make the corners of your lines squared off instead of rounded.

- **Stabilizing**: This option sets the smoothness of the line. The amount of correction is based on the number here; a larger number will smooth the line out more. A smaller one will keep the line closer to how you draw it. Checking the **Correct by speed** option will correct based on how quickly you draw the line. A faster motion will smooth the line more. The circle on the left was drawn with no stabilizing, so it is much closer to the marks actually made by the stylus. The circle on the right had the stabilizing turned up higher, so it's a much smoother line as you can see.

- **Post correction**: Using this option, the line is corrected after it's drawn. I like to have this set to **100** for when I'm working on cityscapes because it will give straight lines, so that saves time. **Adjust by speed** here works the same as the previous option we discussed. **Adjust by display ratio** will do the post correction based on how far you're zoomed in to the canvas. Being zoomed out will produce straighter lines, while being zoomed in will keep the line more as originally drawn, but smooth it a little. Turning the **Bezier curve** option on while working on a vector layer will turn the line into a vector curve that you can adjust later.

- **Brush stroke**: This option automatically thins out the end of the brush stroke. The amount depends on the setting of your slider. This setting can be very handy, especially for getting nice ink lines, but I've found that setting it up to a very high number can produce lines that lag and that continue even after I've picked up my tablet pen.

- **Able to snap**: A tool without this box checked will not snap, even to a ruler that is active.

- **Vector magnet**: When working on a vector layer, this option will snap a vector line with a nearby line and combine them into one line if applicable.

Starting and Ending menu

These options affect the beginning and end of a tool stroke. They are as follows:

- **Starting and Ending**: The dropdown here allows you to set different factors that will be adjusted at the beginning and end of your brush stroke. You can set the size, paint density, and particle sizes and the amount of each that will be adjusted.

- **Methods**: This dropdown has the different ways that the start and end can be affected. Setting to **By length** will adjust based on the length of the brush stroke. Percentage starts at 0 percent at the beginning of the stroke, goes all the way to 100 percent at the middle, then back to 0 percent, regardless of the length of the brush stroke. Setting to **Fade** makes the adjustment gradually increase to the minimum setting from the beginning of the stroke.

- **Starting**: This option shows how much the beginning of the stroke is affected.

- **Ending**: This option shows how much the termination of the stroke is affected. The speed lines in the following screenshot have the starting value set higher than the ending value, giving them a much more tapered beginning of the line on the left, where the stroke begins, than on the side where it ends.

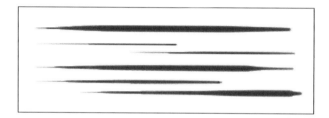

- **Starting and Ending by speed**: This applies the effect based on the speed of the pen movement.

Anti-overflow menu

The anti-overflow options are new to Manga Studio 5, and they are a huge time-saver if you use them! Anti-overflow takes a layer that you have set as a reference layer and will apply it to what the tool you're using is doing on another layer. Let's say that we've finished drawing and inking, and now we're going to put a new layer in our file and do some base colors. Set the ink layer to the reference layer by using the lighthouse icon on the **Layers** palette.

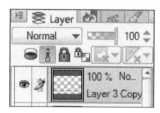

Now we can make a new layer called `Base color`. Turning on the anti-overflow options in your **Sub tool detail** menu will then make the lines for your reference layer in the boundaries of your base color layer. The following screenshots are two examples of this. The top rectangle has purple added beneath it with a pen tool and without the anti-overflow option turned on. The second rectangle has the anti-overflow option on.

Because we had the anti-overflow option on in the second rectangle, the pen tool we used didn't go outside the line of the rectangle.

The other options underneath the anti-overflow menu are as follows:

- **Stop filling at center line of vector**: This option stops the fill at the center line of a vector layer, if vectors are being used.

- **Color margin**: This adjusts the margin of error, or how many colors are included as part of the center line. It also makes the edges of aliased lines (shades of gray instead of straight black) get included in the line of the new fill.

- **Area Scaling**: It shows how much larger or smaller the area that the fill is than the area of the line. Make this a little larger for base color layers, as it will then "seep" the edge of the color under the line layer so that there is no halo effect around the fill.

Importing and exporting your tools

Sharing the tools that you make is a great way to promote your work, or even to make some extra money by selling the tools that you've created! Ray Frenden, of `Frenden.com`, is a very talented artist who uses his site to both promote his work and to share his wonderful Manga Studio brushes. Sometimes he offers his creations as a free download, but you can also buy packages of his brushes to use in your work. He focuses on recreating traditional looking media, and also on dynamic inking pens.

In this section we're going to learn how to export and import our tools. This process is very simple and allows you to take your creations to different computers or share them with other Manga Studio 5 users.

Let's start by exporting our `Sketching Pencil` that we made at the beginning of this chapter. To do this, simply select your pencil tool, and then your **Sketching Pencil** sub tool if it's not already selected. Now, right-click on `Sketching Pencil`.

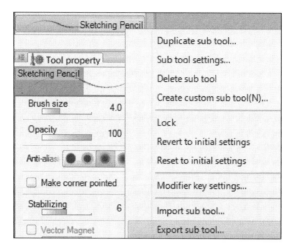

By now you should be familiar with this menu since it's the same one we use to start creating custom tools! Click on **Export sub tool...** in the menu. A **Save** dialog box will come up, and by default our file name will be `Sketching Pencil. sut`. Navigate to a folder where you would like to save your tool, and click on **Save** to complete the process.

> Save all your custom tools in one directory. It will make them easy to find, and you can simply store that folder on a thumb drive or in a cloud storage system to take your tools with you wherever you go!

Importing sub tools is just as easy as exporting. There are two different ways that importing can be done. If you only have to import one or two tools, you can simply right-click in the sub tool menu where you wish to place your tool and click on the **Import sub tool...** option. Navigate to the folder where your `.sut` file is and click on the **Open** button. Your sub tool will be imported into the menu.

However, there is another way to import your tools, and even import multiple sub tools to the same menu at one time. In order to use this method, you need to open the folder where your sub tool files are stored. As you can see in the image, I have all the drawing tools that we've created in this chapter, as well as two new gradient tools that were made on another computer in one folder. I want to import these gradient sub tools to Manga Studio 5, and rather than do one at a time, we're going to import both at once.

With the **Gradation** sub tool menu open, we'll select both the .sut files that we wish to import in the folder where they are stored. Make sure that you can see the Manga Studio window behind your folder! Then click and drag the .sut files into the sub tools menu. The cursor will have a plus sign next to it when you're in the correct spot. Release the mouse button.

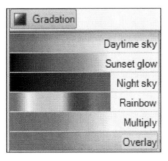

Using this method, you can import many tools to the same sub tool menu at once. It's easy, and it's fast—which is exactly what we want!

Summary

Now you know the basics of creating your own custom tools, so you can customize the look and feel of your drawings in Manga Studio. Here's what we covered in this chapter:

- Using materials and texture to make a pencil tool for sketching
- Adjusting the brush size dynamics, correction, and starting and ending options for crisp ink lines
- Creating a custom material to use as brush tips
- How to use the Mix ground color options to achieve smooth, paint-like gradients between shades of color
- What the drawing sub tool options do and how to use them to create different effects
- Sharing your tools with others, and importing custom tools to your copy of Manga Studio 5

3
Palettes of a Different Color

Color! It's something that Manga Studio in the past has been criticized over. Previous versions of Manga Studio concentrated on black-and-white and grayscale art and weren't intuitive to color in. Smith Micro listened to the Manga Studio fans though, and MS5 and EX5 are now built so that it's a cinch to do all your penciling, inking, and coloring in one program.

In my time as an artist on the Internet, I can't count the number of times that I've seen a character design sheet that had a bunch of dots on it to show the base colors of a character. There's nothing wrong with putting base colors on a character reference sheet, of course, but only so long as you do it correctly. Can you remember what each color goes to? Is that blue for the eyes, or for the detailing on the shirt? Are the base color references on a separate layer so they aren't in the way of your good, finished art, or have you put them on the color layers or the ink layer and now you have to waste time erasing them before you can show off the finished piece?

However, in practice using this method to store your character's base colors can become bogged down and actually cost you more time than it's worth. For one thing, you need to have at least two files open—the file with the palette of dots and the file that you're currently working on. Let's say the above character was the main protagonist in the comic that we were drawing and this was her character design sheet. Storing her base colors strictly like this, as I said, is all well and good. But every time we color her, we'll have to have her character sheet open to pick the colors off. Not only that, but we'll have to switch back and forth between the design sheet and the latest page that we're working on. We'll have to switch to the eyedropper tool every time we pick up a new color (or hold down *Alt* while using one of the drawing tools to bring up the eyedropper, either way that we decide to work). These little steps don't take too long when you're only doing them once or twice. But imagine doing it over and over again, that can add a lot of time to what you're working on! And we're trying to make the process more streamlined and efficient by using the features of Manga Studio.

So, that's why I'm devoting a short chapter to making custom color palettes. It's far easier to switch color sets in Manga Studio 5 than it is to switch between files and tools and color pick off a design sheet. Two clicks of a mouse will let you switch color sets, and while they do take some time to set up initially, once you have them put together they're an invaluable resource. You can organize them by skin tones, hair colors, colors of a similar tone, or put together palettes based on a specific comic or a set of characters. It's up to you how you want to use the program. But I'll show you how to use the custom color sets so that you can figure out what works best for you.

Let's get started!

Using the preset palettes

Manga Studio 5 has many ways to pick colors other than using the color sets. We'll take a look at these as we look at the color sets, so that you're familiar with all the options and can use them to your advantage.

Color circle

We'll start with the **Color circle** menu, which you can locate by default on the left-hand side of Manga Studio 5 at the bottom. If you don't see it, simply go to the **Window** menu at the top of the screen and then select the **Color circle** option. This will bring up the appropriate menu. The color circle is—appropriately enough—a circle with a slider outside of either a square or a triangle. The outside slider controls the overall hue, while the inside square or triangle allows you to pick more or less intense or saturated variations of the chosen hue.

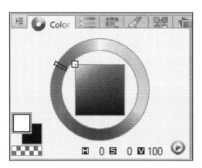

If there is a square in the center of your circle, then you are on the Hue, Saturation, and Value (HSV) color space. Clicking on the circle and triangle icon in the bottom right of the **Color circle** tab will switch to the Hue, Lightness, and Saturation (HLS) color space. These are just methods of picking colors and we really don't have to be too concerned with the differences between them so long as you're comfortable with whatever method you decide to use.

To the left of the icon that we just used to change the color space model are three numbers. Clicking in this area will switch between the HSV or HLS numbers, or the Red, Green, and Blue (RGB) numbers. If you have a color in Manga Studio that you need to take to another application, these numbers will help you get the same shade again.

The far left bottom corner icons allow you to change the foreground or background color. In the previous screenshot, the white square is your foreground color and the black square is your background color. The white square is highlighted, indicating that it is currently active. If you wish to change the background color, simply click on the background box to highlight it, then select a new color.

Color slider

To bring up the **Color slider** menu, either click the tab with three horizontal bars at the top of the **Color palette** window, or navigate to **Window | Color slider**. You have options for how to pick colors here too, and can control whether you are changing the foreground or background color with the boxes below the slider bars. Using a color system like this, to me, has always seemed more laborious than it needs to be. But if you need precise control over your colors, this is the way to get it. The default slider is RGB, and you can either use the triangles under each bar to adjust the color, or use the up and down arrows to the right of the numbers for more precise adjustments.

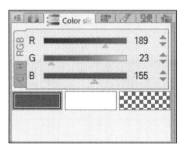

The tabs on the left of the **Color slider** menu allow you to switch between different color models. Clicking on the tab with the letter **H** visible brings up the HSV color space that we talked about in the previous section. HSV also has sliders and up and down arrows for adjusting your color selection.

The final tab on the left-hand side is CMYK, which is the color model used in printing. When you print something, the inks used are cyan, magenta, yellow, and black. It is the layering of these inks that creates all the other colors that can be printed. Using CMYK color modes produces more true-to-life prints since what you see on the screen will be a close approximation to what is printed.

Mix color

The fifth tab of the **Color palette** window is called **Mix color**, and of course you can get there by navigating to **Window | Mix color**. At first glance, this method of picking colors might seem a bit intimidating, but it's really not hard at all! In fact, if you have any experience with mixing paint, this method is the one most like that. The four large boxes at the corners of the grid are where you put the colors that you wish to mix. As the colors get further from their own corners, they become a blend of the color that they are heading toward. The colors in the center of the grid are a mixture of the four corner squares.

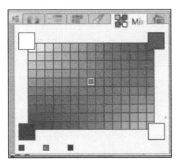

As you can see in the previous screenshot, the colors along the top row of the grid go from white to pink and then to red. Down the right side the colors transition from red to orange, and then to yellow as they get to the yellow corner. Along the bottom there is a gradient from yellow to purple. Then up the left-hand side the grid goes from purple to lilac and then back to white. The very center of the grid is a pale rose color, created by mixing the four corners together. If we were to replace the white square with black, we would get a very different color, as you can see in the following screenshot:

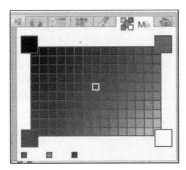

Now we have much deeper, darker colors because we're adding black instead of white. Using this method is best for creating harmonious color schemes.

 Want to create tons of skin tone variation in a flash? Use the **Mix color** tab! Select your skin base tone as one corner, the shadow color as another, and the highlight as a third. You can also put an accent color in the fourth square, for colored or reflected light! In this example, my base color is in the top-left, the shadow color is in the bottom left. The top-right square is my skin highlight color and the bottom right is a blue contrast color.

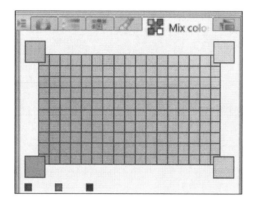

Approx. color

The right-most tab in the **Color palette** window is the **Approx. color** screen. This looks quite a bit like the **Mix color** tab that we just discussed. However, instead of four squares that allow us to mix colors in the center, this screen has sliders on the left and top side that allow you to change the value of the grid squares. Either of these sliders can be changed simply by clicking on the text next to the slide bar and selecting from the menu. The example image has the left-side of the grid set to hue (**H**), while the top of the grid is set to saturation (**S**). Changing these sliders allows us to adjust the colors of the swatches within the grid.

For instance, if we drag the saturation from 100 percent down to 0 percent, we will create paler, more muted colors. The hue slider being taken from 100 percent to 0 percent gives us less choices of hue—going from the entire spectrum to a monochromatic scheme instead.

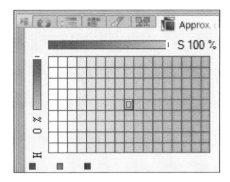

The best way to figure out what all these options do is really to play with them. Try changing each of the two sliders to a different option by clicking on the text next to them, and then dragging the values to see the differences. Personally, I rather think that the rainbow of colors given by setting each one to hue 100 percent is quite pleasing! But it might make for a jarring color palette for a finished image.

Color set

Now we're going to look at the color sets, which is where you can make and save palettes of color to use in your art. Click on the third tab in the **Color palette** window, or navigate to **Window | Color set**. You should see a grid with colors in it, and above that a drop-down menu along with a wrench icon.

Manga Studio 5 comes with many pre-made color sets. The **Default color set** palette has 128 color swatches that are suited for general purpose, fast color selections. Think of this as a big box of crayons that you had as a child! It had plenty of colors to color just about anything, but you had to be creative if you wanted a slightly different tone and didn't have it, right? Luckily with Manga Studio we can make any color, even if we elect to use the **Default color set** palette most of the time.

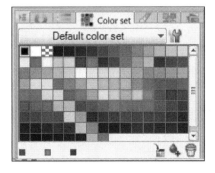

The **Default color set** palette is just one of the sets that come loaded in Manga Studio 5. Clicking on the drop-down menu will bring up the list of pre-loaded palettes that you can choose from. There is an **Additional color set** palette, which is much like the **Default color set** palette but with far more colors to choose from. Then there are sets that are broken down into tones, which is very handy if you're going for a specific mood in a page or illustration. Say that you wanted to do a scene that was dark and unsaturated; you could use the **DarkTone** or **DullTone** palettes to pick your base colors. The **BrightTone** and **VividTone** palettes give a much more saturated look, of course. These color sets are a fine starting-off point for setting the mood of your colored illustration or comic page.

 Even if you use the presets to make picking colors fast and easy, you can still create any shades that you want. Choose a color from the sets that's close to what you want, then go over to the **Color circle** or the **Color slider** tabs and adjust to your tastes.

Editing existing color sets

Not only can you add custom colors to existing sets, but you can also rename sets and reorder them in the drop-down menu as well. This allows you to put all your most used colors, or sets of colors, where it's most convenient for you to get to them quickly.

In order to illustrate the ways that you can add or replace colors in existing sets, we're going to need to pick some custom colors. To make this easier to illustrate, I've decided to pull the **Color set** tab out and place it beside the **Color circle** tab. While you're following along, you can just switch back and forth between the tabs if you'd like.

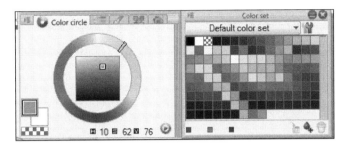

Adding or replacing colors is very easy. Let's make a nice, medium-green shade, and then let's say that we really like this shade and we want to save it to the defaults because we're going to be using it more often. You will note that at the bottom of the **Color set** tab, there is an icon that looks like a droplet with a plus sign next to it. This is the icon to add color. The new green shade will be added to the bottom of our **Color set**.

Great! As you can see, our green is now at the bottom of our **Default color set**. Well, what if we decided that we no longer liked this green? Maybe we made a mistake, and the color for this character was supposed to be pink instead? We can simply select the color that we no longer want and click on the trash can icon to the right of the add color icon.

Or, we can replace the color that we no longer want with another color. Select the green shade that we just added to the color set. Now, using the **Color circle** tab, let's make a pink shade instead. Once you're happy with your color, click on the icon to the left of the add color icon, the one that has an arrow pointing down to the grid (that looks a lot like our color set, doesn't it?).

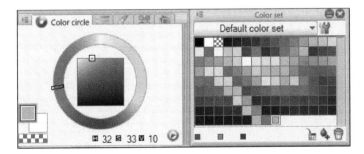

The new pink color has overridden our green shade, rather than being added in addition to the color we had there earlier. So, if some of the colors in the default color set don't suit you, you could always replace them with colors that you like better and that fit the needs of your projects.

We can also rename the color sets and pick what order they'll be listed in the drop-down menu. To do this, you'll need to click on the icon that looks like a wrench next to the drop-down menu with the color set name. This brings up the **Edit color set** menu, where we can create and manage our color sets.

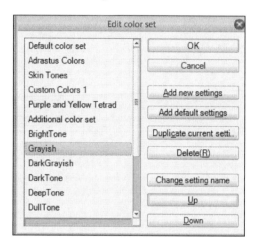

Let's rearrange our color sets before we make a brand new set. Let's move the set titled **Grayish** up to the top of the list. Select the **Grayish** color set from the list of sets and then click on the button to the right labeled **Up**. The color set name will move up in the list. Keep clicking on the **Up** button until the **Grayish** set is at the very top. To move it back down, simply make sure that the set you wish to relocate is selected and then click on the **Down** button.

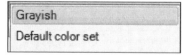

If you wish to rename a set in the list, select it and click on the **Change setting name** button. Enter a new name, and then press the *Enter* key on your keyboard. These are the basics of working with the existing color sets, so now let's make some sets of our own to use on our characters!

Making new color sets

While we're still on the **Edit color set** menu, let's go ahead and make a new set with our own custom swatches! There are four buttons in the middle right of this menu that will assist us in doing just that. The button labeled **Add new settings** will give us a brand new, shiny, blank set of swatches to fill up. **Add default settings** will give us a copy of the default color set, which is very handy if you want to use most of the colors from the default palette and edit a few to fit your tastes.

Duplicate current settings creates a copy of whatever color set is currently selected. Say you liked the **DeepTone** set but wanted to add more colors to it without affecting the original set. You could duplicate the set and make changes to the copy instead.

Delete(R) will erase your currently selected settings.

 Deleting your color set has no confirmation, so make sure that it's what you really want to do before you click on the **Delete(R)** button!

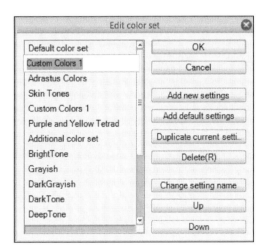

Alright, let's make ourselves a color set! Click on the **Add new settings** button and a new entry will be created in our list of settings. Let's name this Custom Colors 1. Then click on **OK** on the **Edit color set** menu. The menu will close and we now have a set of empty swatches just waiting for color. Empty swatches are marked by the white-and-gray checkerboard pattern.

Open a picture off which you want to make a set of colors, or you can follow along with the color palette that I've put together at `http://adrastuscomic.com/wp-content/uploads/2013/07/colors.png`. If you choose to do this, either save the image to your hard drive and open it in Manga Studio, or right-click and copy the image and paste it into your opened page in Manga Studio. When you're done building your color set, you can delete the color swatch image and continue using the canvas.

Now that we have an empty set to work on and a color palette to pick from, let's start customizing. You can lay out your colors however you wish, but I usually use one row per character and go from the top (their hair color) to the bottom (their shoe color). Ideally my sets will be organized in the following order, going horizontally:

- Hair base color
- Hair secondary color, if applicable
- Skin base color
- Eye base color
- Shirt base color
- Shirt secondary color, if applicable
- Accessories colors
- Pants or skirt color
- Pants or skirt secondary color, if applicable
- Shoes

Of course different characters will have different numbers of base colors; some may require more or less swatches, but this is approximately the process that I have to organize my sets so that I know which color goes where on the character.

If you're following along with the image that I've provided, you can simply go horizontally across each row and select the colors. If you are working off your own drawing or photograph, I'll let you decide the best way to organize your colors. Whatever works best for you is the best way to do it after all!

I find this easiest to do if I actually use the eyedropper tool while I'm picking my colors up to save them. If you have one of the drawing tools selected though, you can hold down the *Alt* key on your keyboard as a hotkey to pull up the eyedropper temporarily. It will switch back to whatever drawing tool you have selected once you release the *Alt* key.

Click in the first empty square of the new color set we created to make it active. Then use the eyedropper tool to select your first color from your image. Use either the replace color or add color icon at the bottom of the **Color set** tab to save your selection. To save your next color, click in the next empty square that you wish to fill, use your eyedropper tool to select your color, and then either add or replace color again.

 To add, or to replace, that is the question. If you use the add color icon, Manga Studio will create an additional square to place your new color in. So if you use this option then you may end up with a bunch of empty spots on your color set that you need to delete—unless you want to leave them there. Replace color will fill the selected empty square in the grid without creating a new square, so you still end up with the same amount of available squares. This is my method, personally, but that's because I like to keep things organized!

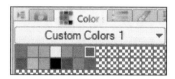

Continue until you've saved all the colors that you wish to access later on. As you can see in the previous screenshot, I've broken each line into the characters that the colors belong to, starting with the main character's colors and working down from there. You could give each character their own set if you wanted, or even sets for different environments if that's how you prefer to work. I have a color set for the characters from my webcomic, and I also have a set of nothing but skin tones and colors that complement those skin tones as well, for when I'm working on other projects. How you organize things is up to you, but later on when you're working, it will be much easier to pick your base colors this way than it will be to switch back and forth between character design sheets or previous pages!

Summary

So in this chapter you've learned:

- The importance of saving custom sets of colors
- How custom sets can speed up your workflow in the long run
- Ways to interact with already existing sets of colors
- How to create your own color sets

These custom swatches are going to be a big help to us. Let's move on to the next chapter, shall we?

4

Setting up Your Space

Having your workspace set up to facilitate the way that you draw can help you save time and a whole lot of effort. After all, if you're a lefty like me, you don't want to have to reach across your drawing every time you need one of your most used tools. Though this isn't much of an issue if you're using a traditional digital tablet, onscreen drawing tablets are becoming more and more popular and affordable. In this chapter we will explore different ways of setting up the Manga Studio workspace, so that you can optimize your flow and always have your tools right where you can reach them. Topics covered will include:

- Moving palette windows
- Left- and right-handed workspaces
- Registering your custom workspace
- Switching between saved workspaces

Moving things around

Rearranging your screen in Manga Studio is really easy. But I think that being able to customize things so that they fit your workflow and make getting to your frequently used tools easier is more efficient. Lots of software users don't think about changing where their tools are located, but it can really help. Especially if you are left-handed, or even disabled in some way, you can set the program so that it works best for the way that you create your comics.

So more of this chapter is going to be on why I would pick certain locations for tools and palettes, and less on how to get them there, because getting things to new locations really isn't hard. But if you don't set up your screen in a way that's convenient to you in the beginning, then you're just going to waste more time getting to your tools later. It may take a little experimenting to get your things all where you like them, so don't be afraid to experiment and try something new.

Alright, let's try some moving and see how we can optimize this screen! But first, let's look at what the default positions are for everything just so that we can know where everything currently is. That way we can plan where we're going to move things to.

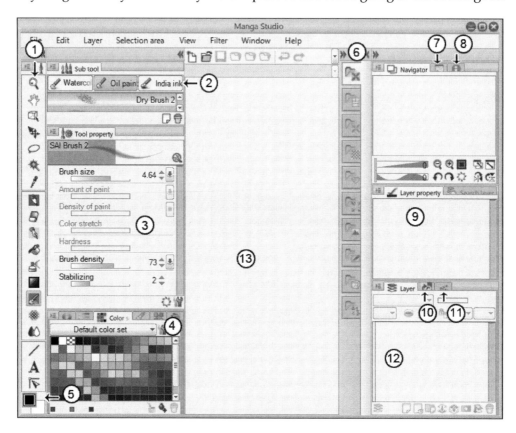

The elements seen on the Manga Studio screen are as follows:

1. Toolbar
2. Sub tools
3. Tool property
4. Color sets
5. Active foreground and background colors
6. Materials palette
7. Sub-view palette

8. System info palette
9. Layer properties
10. History palette
11. Auto action palette
12. Layers palette
13. Canvas area

Nearly everything on this screen can be moved around to customize your Manga Studio experience. Let's say that we want to have our pencil tool, pen tool, and eraser at the top of our toolbox instead of the zoom, hand, and select object tools. Left-click on your pencil tool and drag it up to the top of the toolbox, then release your mouse button. Do the same for the pen and eraser tool. When you drag the tools around you will see a red line that will indicate where you are about to release the icon. Use this to ensure that your placement is where you want it.

Moving the palette windows around follows the same approach: simply click and drag the tab to where you want to reposition it. Let's switch the **Sub tool** and **Color sets** tabs on the left-hand side of the screen.

While moving my **Color window** tabs from the bottom to the top of the screen, I decided to reorganize them too. Since I use the **Color sets** and the **Color circle** the most, I put those first, and moved the **Brush sizes** tab so that it wasn't in the middle of all those color ones. It seemed silly to me, to not put all the ways to choose colors together and have the brush sizes tab in the middle of them!

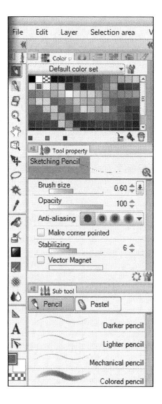

Let's also relocate the **Materials** menu from the right-hand to the left-hand side of the screen. Left-click on the gray section between the arrows at the top of the **Materials** menu and drag it. You can dock the **Materials** either to the right or left of the sub tool palettes. You can even dock it to the far left or right of the screen if you want. Though if you do, it will cover up the toolbox on the left side of the screen or part of the windows on the right side of the screen.

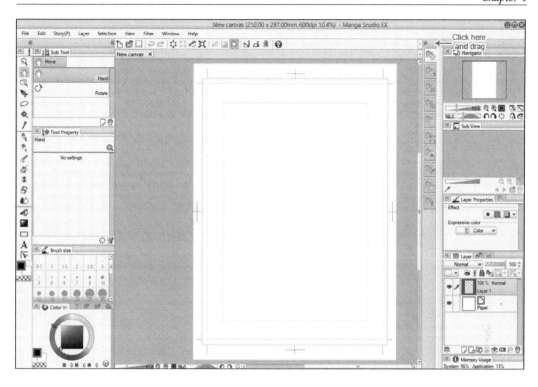

The preceding screenshot shows the **Material** window docked all the way to the left of the screen, covering the **Toolbox** window:

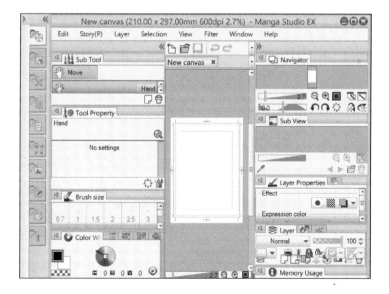

The preceding screenshot shows the **Material** window docked to the right of the toolbox, between it and the Sub tool menus:

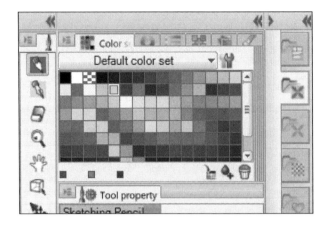

The preceding screenshot shows the **Material** window docked to the right side of the color set and tool property windows, between them and the canvas window:

The preceding screenshot shows the **Materials** window docked to the right of the navigator and layers windows.

If you don't want to see a certain section of palettes at all, you can close and reopen sections of the screen at will. Say that you're currently sketching on a layer and don't need your Layers palette or a lot of brush options. You just need your pencil tool and want to be able to draw and have as much access to the canvas as you need. Clicking on the double arrows at the top of any of the sections of palettes will close them, and then clicking on the double arrows again will open them back up when you need them again.

In order to hide all of the palette windows and toolbars at once, simply hit the *Tab* key on your keyboard. This can be very helpful if you don't have a lot of screen space and want to maximize how much of your image you can see and work on at once. When you need your tools and palettes again, hit *Tab* once more and they will reappear.

If you've used Manga Studio 3 or 4, then you're familiar with the floating windows that were used in those versions, rather than the palettes being docked. The good thing is that you can pull any of your palettes out of the docks and have them floating if you'd like. Let's do this with the **Navigator** palette. Simply left-click and drag the palette until it is over the canvas, then release the mouse button.

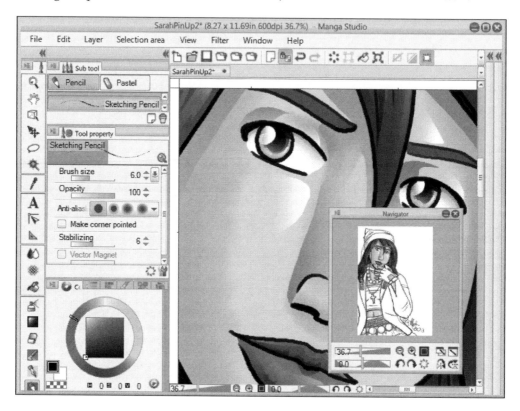

Customizing the Command Bar

Other than the positions of the various palettes, another thing that can be customized and saved among workspaces is the **Command Bar** menu at the top of the screen, the units of measurement, and the keyboard shortcuts.

Personalizing the **Command Bar** is a great way to add icons for operations that you use often. In fact, let's add making a **New Raster Layer** to the **Command Bar** so that you can see what I mean. To edit your **Command Bar**, go to **File | Command bar settings**.

Anything that you can access from the menu at the very top of Manga Studio can be added to the **Command Bar** over the top of the canvas. You'll see a list of categories under a preview of the **Command Bar**. Clicking on the triangles to the left of the category name will open it and show you the options under it. Functions that are already added to the **Command Bar** cannot be added again.

Click on the triangle next to the **Layer** category and select the **New Raster Layer** entry.

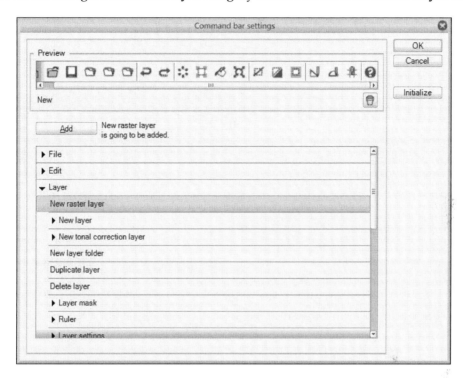

Once we select a command that isn't already in the **Command Bar**, the **Add** button above the category list will become active, and there will be a prompt next to it telling us that the command will be added. Click on **Add** and a new icon will appear in the preview section.

Now we can drag this icon to wherever we would like to place it. Let's drag the **New Raster Layer** icon over to the right and put it with the **Ruler Snap** icons.

Let's also get rid of the **Manga Studio Help** icon, so that we can see how to delete an icon from the **Command Bar**. The **Help** icon is the question mark in the circle all the way to the right side. Click on it and then click on the trash can icon under the preview window. Manga Studio will prompt that this icon is about to be deleted and then ask if you're sure you want to proceed. If you are, go ahead and click on **Delete**.

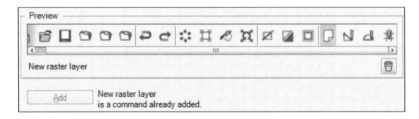

Once you have your icon shortcuts set up the way that you want them, click on the **OK** button. Your new icon will appear at the top of the screen once the dialog box has disappeared!

Note that the **Initialize** button on the **Command bar settings** window is actually the button to use in order to revert back to the settings that Manga Studio was installed with. So, if for any reason you find that you want to go back to the original set up, simply click on this button!

Left- and right-handed setups

Of course, how you set up your space is going to depend heavily on how you work, what tools you commonly use, and what features you regularly need to access. It's very possible that the default Manga Studio layout is perfect for you, and if so that's great. But I find that having my tools where it's convenient for me to access them helps me speed along my work a lot. And when you're trying to do a lot of comic pages, that little bit of extra time not spent reaching across your tablet to switch tools can add up a lot.

We're going to assume for now that you have a graphics tablet that doesn't have a screen in it like a Cintiq, so a regular Wacom Bamboo. After we set up for a lefty with a regular graphics tablet then we'll set up for a lefty that's drawing on the screen. And don't worry, righties, we won't leave you out!

Left-handed setup for regular tablets

The nice thing about working with a tablet that doesn't allow you to draw directly on the screen is that you don't have your hand in the way of what you're doing. It's less intuitive, and requires far more hand-eye coordination, but you don't have anything in the way of your art.

So, with a left-handed setup we're going to put our important items on the left side of the screen, where they're easiest to get to. For the sake of this layout, let's say that we don't use the **Tool Property** menu a lot, but that we often switch layers. With that in mind, let's switch around the positions of the **Tool Property** and **Layers** menus.

First of all we're going to ensure that our layout is back at its default settings. Any time that you want to reset to the default layout, simply go to **Window | Workspace | Back to Default Layout**.

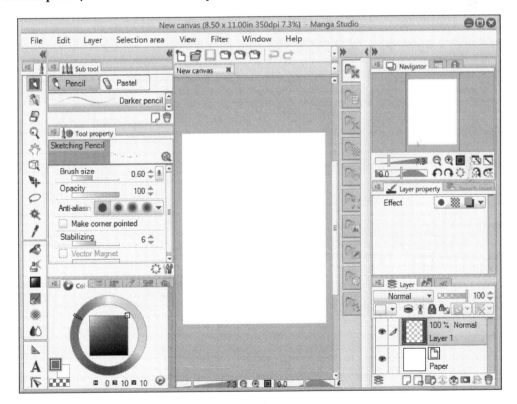

This command will only change palette position modifications. It will not affect the toolbox. As you can see in the screenshot, the locations of my palettes are back to the default, but the Pencil, Pen, and Eraser tools are still at the top of the Toolbox, which is where we moved them to in the previous section.

So the tool properties and the layers palettes are now going to switch. You can either move the layers first and then the tool properties, or the other way around. It doesn't matter so long as eventually you get things the way you want them!

We're also going to want more access to the **History** and **Actions** tabs that are currently now behind the **Tool Property** tab. So let's pull those out and give them their own window instead of being tabs within another window. Simply click and drag one of them until there's a red horizontal line across the right side of the windows.

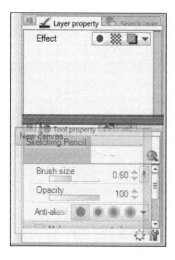

Once we have the **History** and **Auto-action** palettes moved out from the **Tool Properties** section, we can resize the palettes to make it easier to see everything. Move your mouse over the line separating our new palette window from the **Layer Property** window until it becomes an arrow that's pointing up and down. Then simply click and drag up to make the **Layer Property** palette smaller and give our **History** and **Auto-action** palettes some room to breathe.

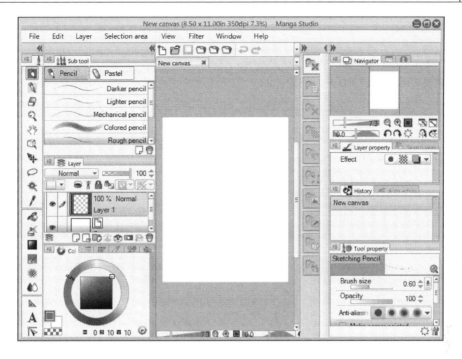

Now let's register this workspace so that we can come back to it later. Registering the workspace saves your window placements so that you can continue to move things around but then come back to previous settings that you've had.

To register your workspace, go to **Window | Layout | Register Workspace**. Since this is the space that we set up for a lefty working with a traditional (not drawing on screen) graphics tablet, let's choose the name `Left Hand Trad Tablet`.

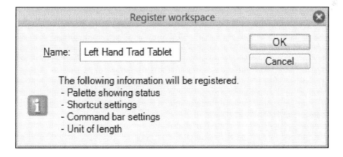

As you can see from the text about what will be registered, you can even have workspaces that are set to **millimeters** (**MM**) instead of **pixels** (**PX**). Maybe for some projects you need to work in one instead of the other. Rather than manually switching your preferences, you could set up a workspace for the project that requires MM measurements and then just load it when you work on that comic.

Left-handed setup for onscreen drawing tablets

I really love being able to draw directly on a screen. It feels most like drawing on a paper, with the ease and convenience that I've come to expect from digital drawing. Unfortunately, it does come with its own share of inconveniences—one being smudges on the screen from my hands!

One of the biggest problems that I have on my own drawing screen is that sometimes my hand covers something that I'm looking at. This is especially an issue when I'm selecting tools and scrolling through the materials menu, because I can't easily see what I'm looking at. We're going to solve this problem with a customized layout that will make it easier for the left-handed user with an onscreen drawing tablet to navigate through the software and find their tools.

Another thing that we need to consider when setting up for drawing on the screen is whether the top or bottom of the screen is easier to reach. Personally, for me, I have my screen at quite an angle, so the bottom of the screen is actually easier for me to get to because I don't have to lift my arm quite so much. Alternatively, you might use your tablet flat or hold it differently and prefer having your most used features at the top of the screen. All of this is based on preference and how you like to work, so again feel free to switch anything around to a place where it works best for you!

Here are my suggestions for a left-handed workspace, on a screen directly. You'll note that I've kept the toolbox where it is, but have moved the **Layer** and **Navigator** palettes to the left. The **Navigator** palette is a handy thing to have within reach when you're zoomed far in on a page and need to jump to another part quickly. Honestly, I never used to use it in any program until I realized just how useful it was, so now I use it a lot to save time. You can also hold down the spacebar to engage the hand tool in order to quickly navigate around your canvas, by the way!

The **Materials** menu has been docked to the left side. This makes it a little easier for the left-handed user to access and see. The scroll bar for navigating the actual materials is still on the right when the menu is accessed, meaning that the hand will cover some of the screen. It's more conveniently placed though than having it on the right side, where the hand would cover a more significant portion of the menu.

The **brush size** tab was moved over to the right side, still accessible but out of the way of things that we'll need more often.

If you look at the toolbox on the left side, you'll see that I also rearranged a lot of the tools. The common drawing tools are now at the bottom of the screen, for ease of reach. A new category has also been created for the **Fill**, **Pattern Brush**, and **Blur** tools.

To create a new category on the toolbox, left-click and drag one of your icons so that it's over the separation between current categories. A horizontal red line will show up, and once you release your mouse button, the new separation will show with your icon inside it. If you wish to undo this, simply drag the icon out of the new category.

Now that we have our second left-handed workspace created, let's register it so that we can come back to it again later. Go to **Window | Workspace | Register Workspace**. Enter a name for your Workspace and hit **OK**, and Manga Studio will save your settings.

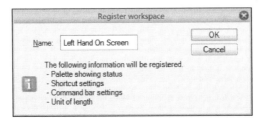

Right-handed setups

Sometimes it would be nice to be right-handed or at least ambidextrous. Being a righty means that you don't have to worry about getting pencil lead or pen ink all over you when you write, for one thing. It also means that most of the world is set up for you already! But there are still a few changes that could make the Manga Studio setup a little more convenient for even the majority of the world's population.

We've kept most of the screen setup the same. But the toolbox has moved to the right side of the screen instead of the left. The **Sub tool** palette has also been moved so that it's above **Navigator**, making it easier to select specific tools.

Of course we're going to register our new workspace. Do this by going to **Window | Workspace | Register Workspace**. Let's name this one `Right Handed`, as that's what it's set up for after all.

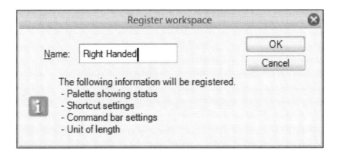

Making a coloring workspace

Now we're going to set up a workspace specifically to use when coloring. I'm going to be honest here, I hated coloring before I began to use Manga Studio 5! MS5 gives me the results I've striven for though without a lot of hassle, and I love that. It's completely changed my mind on coloring.

But, coloring is a different beast than drawing or laying out pages. To really get through a lot of coloring we'll want to maximize the amount of screen that we have access to (how much of the canvas we can see) and make sure that our tools are arranged so that they can be reached quickly. A well set up workspace can save so much time later and make you fly through your artwork faster than before.

Okay, so when I make a new workspace I like to start off at the default Manga Studio layout. To reset any palette layout changes you've made, go to **Window | Workspace | Back to default layout**.

The first thing we're going to do is get the **Materials** out of the way. Clicking on the double arrow will collapse **Materials** down to a small gray bar. Drag the collapsed **Materials** over all the way to the right just to get it to one side. We also won't need the **Memory Information** palette, which is nested with the **Navigator** palette. Click on it to select it. Then, from the icon at the top-left corner of the palette window select **Hide Memory Information Palette**.

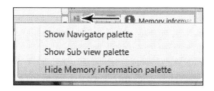

[

Need to bring the palette back? Click on the same icon in the upper left of the palette that it was originally nested in and choose to show it again. Or use the Windows menu at the top of the screen and select the palette that you wish to show.
]

The next thing that we should do is try to clear a little more space on our screen. Looking at the palettes that are still open, I know that I might use the **Layer properties** palette while coloring, but I most likely won't use the **Search Layers** palette. So let's drag **Layer Properties** down to the **Layers** palette and put it between **Layers** and **History**. Then we can hide the **Search Layers** palette as we won't be using it.

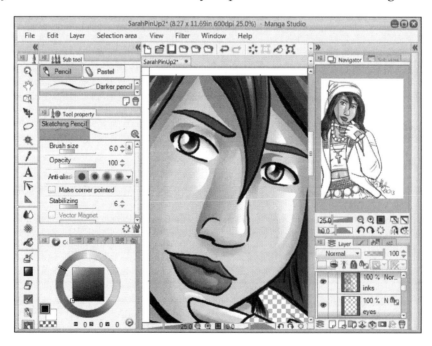

When coloring we'll be accessing the **Layers** more than **Tool property**, so let's switch those around. Clicking in the empty space to the right of the **Auto-action** palette and dragging with the mouse button still held down will move the entire cluster of palettes as a group, which is much easier than moving those four palettes together!

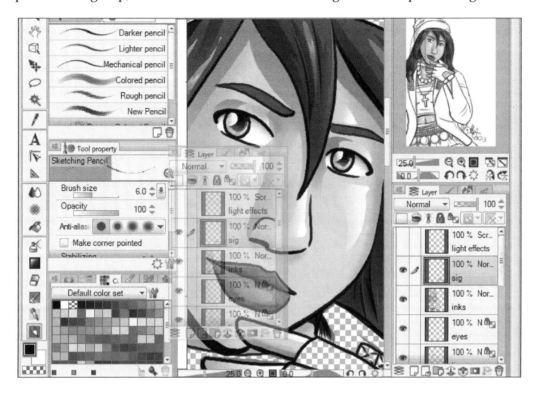

For final touches that just go with how I know that I work, I'm going to relocate the **Brush size** palette from out of the **Color** palettes at the bottom left, and put it with the **Tool property**. Then I like to drag the **Color Sets** to the left so they're the first tab in the color palette.

As one final adjustment, let's add an icon to the **Command Bar** to **Lock Transparent Pixel** on our current layer. Go to **File | Command bar settings**. Under the **Layer** category, expand the **Layer Settings**, and choose the **Lock transparent pixel** command. Then click on the **Add** button and the icon will be added to our **Command Bar**. Once you are done with that, click on **OK**.

Let's go ahead and register our workspace, of course, since we'll want to come back to it later on. Go to **Window | Workspace | Register Workspace**. Since we made this workspace specifically for coloring, we can name it `Coloring`. Enter the name in the text box and click on **OK**.

Here is what we have now for our Coloring setup. This workspace has lots of space on the canvas, easy access to Navigator and the layers, and the layer shortcuts at the top are going to be a big asset while we work.

Switching and managing workspaces

You can rename and delete workspaces by going to **Window | Workspace | Manage Workspace**. This menu will allow you to rename and delete workspaces.

If you need to delete a workspace, click on it to highlight it and then hit the **Delete** button. To rename a workspace, highlight it and then use the **Change setting name** button. Type in a new name and hit Enter on your keyboard. Once you're done taking care of your changes, press the **OK** button.

Switching between our Workspaces is as simple as pressing two mouse buttons. Simply go to **Window | Workspace** and then click on the name of the workspace that you want to use. You might notice that Manga Studio comes with two workspaces already set up, as well. One of these is a **Manga** workspace and the other is called **Illustration**. I'd suggest loading those up and seeing if you like one of them to use for your own work. One of the great things about Manga Studio 5 is that you don't have to make yourself and your workflow work around the program. Instead, have the program work for you!

Summary

Before we move on, let's do a review of what we've learned in this chapter:

- Moving palettes from one dock to another
- Rearranging tabs within a palette
- Making a palette into a floating window
- Closing off docks of palettes to open up screen space
- Adding icons to the **Command Bar** menu
- Setting up workspaces for left- or right-handed users
- Personalizing a space for a specific task like coloring
- Registering workspaces
- Managing your workspaces and switching between them

In the next chapter we will delve into the wild world of **Materials**. So, let's get started!

5
Living in a Material World

There are a lot of different things under the Materials definition in Manga Studio 5. Everything from panel layouts to screentones, images, dialog balloons, and even 3D models can be found in the **Materials** tab. Learning how to use and make materials is a great way to speed along your work. We're going to start exploring them now!

In this chapter we will go over the following topics:

- Using materials and tones
- Navigating and searching materials
- Editing materials
- Making custom materials and speech balloons

Navigating and searching your materials

To bring up the **Materials** window, either open the menu if you still have it docked in your workspace, or go to **Window | Materials** to bring it up.

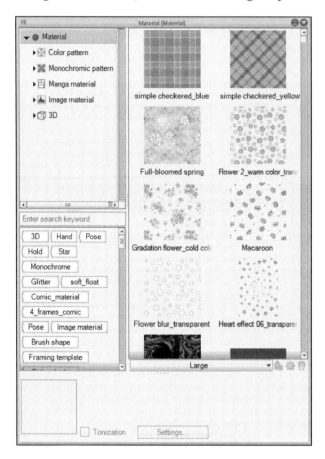

The top menu on the left shows the different categories of materials. Back in *Chapter 2, The Right Tools for the Job*, when we made our Custom Brush tool, one of these categories is where we stored the texture that we made for it:

- **Color pattern**: This consists of materials, including textures and backgrounds, that are in color.

- **Monochromic pattern**: This includes black and white patterns, background, effects, and screentones.

- **Manga material**: This includes panel layout templates, speech balloons, effect lines, and sound effects.

- **Image material**: This includes brush tip images, as well as illustrations and pictures.
- **3D**: This includes 3D models.

To browse through the materials in each section, you can either click on the category name and Manga Studio will allow you to see a preview of every material stored in that folder, or you can click the triangle icon next to the category name and browse by sub-categories. However, a much faster way to find the materials that you want is to use the keywords and search in the menu directly under the categories.

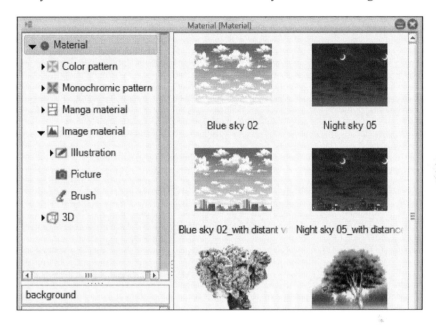

Let's say that we're working on a panel and we want a swirly background, something that will convey a confused emotion for the panel that we're working on. Let's enter the search term background into our search box.

Alright, so entering background as our search term brought up nature and buildings. Not what we're looking for, but that's okay. We'll pick another term and see if we can come up with something closer. Since the emotion that we're looking for is a confused one, let's enter confusion as our search.

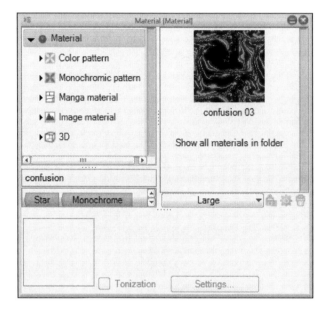

Success! We found a texture that will be perfect for what we want. Now that we have a material picked out, let's add it to our panel. To do that we simply left-click on the thumbnail in the right-hand side of the **Material** window and drag it to our panel. Release the mouse and the material will be dropped onto its own layer in the image.

If you need to resize or rotate the material, you can do so using the light-blue handles around the edge of the material. You may need to zoom out to see them, depending on the dimensions of the material and your canvas.

We can also find a material that we wish to add by clicking on one or more of the tags that show in the Search window. For instance, let's say that we want to add a pre-existing speech balloon to this panel. Rather than use the balloon tool, we'll find one in the materials instead.

First, make sure that your search terms are cleared and that you have clicked on the top **Materials** folder. If you have the **Monochromic pattern** folder or another sub-folder selected, your search will only pull tagged material from that folder. Right now we want to search all the material, so click on the top folder.

Next we're going to pick some tags from the search window. Click on the **Comic_ material** tag (the box around the tag will turn blue) and Manga Studio will display every material with this as a tag, including framing templates and effect lines. Let's try also selecting the **Monochrome** tag and see if that will narrow our search down.

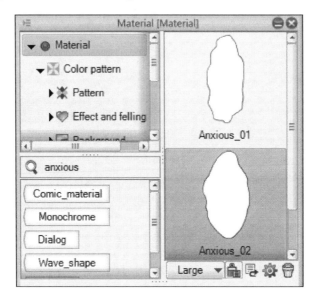

Now you'll see only materials tagged with these two keywords, and dialog balloons are at the top of our list. Let's select **Anxious_02** to add to our scene here. Select it and drag it to your canvas or you can click on your material and then click on the icon that looks like a clipboard to insert the material as well.

Position and resize your balloon to where you want it. Then we'll add some text using the text tool. Select the text tool, click with it inside your balloon and type whatever you want your character to say. Manga Studio will automatically partner your new text with the dialog material so that you can move both items as one element from now on, just in case you need to rearrange a page or shift your text somewhere, so that you don't need to waste time shifting both the text and the material.

We can also search the **Materials** under a sub-category. Let's open the **Color pattern** folder and then choose the **Pattern** sub-category. Either enter `Flower` in the Search box or click on the **Flower** tag to highlight it. Now the only materials that we will see are the ones tagged with **Flower** in the **Color pattern** category.

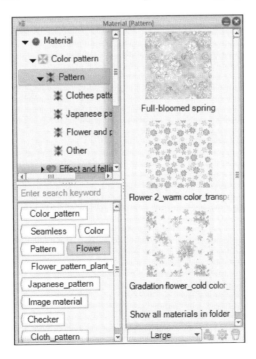

But if we click back on the top **Material** folder and then search for Flower, we will get more results because there are materials tagged with Flower in other folders. For instance, the Cherry Blossom image is tagged with **Color, Flower**, but it is stored in the **Image material, Brush shape** category, so it did not come up when we searched just in the **Color patterns**.

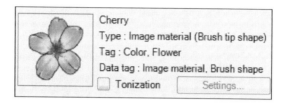

Editing materials

Okay, so now that we know how to search through what's already there, let's learn how to edit and add our own tags and other settings.

For instance, let's go back to the confusion material that we used in the first section for the background of our panel. Remember how when we searched for background, it didn't show up because it hasn't been tagged as a background? We're going to change that right now.

First pull up the **Materials** window and search for Confusion. The swirled black and purple image that we used before will come up again. Select it by clicking on it to highlight it.

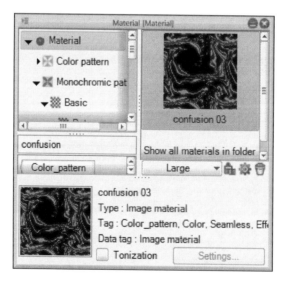

The text at the bottom of the materials window shows us the name of the material, what type it is (what folder it's stored in), the tags, and the data tag. To edit these options and more, we can either click on the Gear icon underneath the search results, or double-click on the thumbnail of the material we're going to edit.

Once you click on the gear you will see the **Material property** window. This is where we can change all the data about a material, even its name. Let's make some edits and customize this material so that it works the way we want it to, and so that we can find it easily the next time that we're looking for it.

First let's change the name of the material. Right now, it's **confusion 03**. Let's pick something a little more descriptive than that. How about *Swirly Confusion*? You can enter any name that you'd like, but I'm going to use this one. Underneath the material name you'll see a preview of the material. Then beneath the thumbnail there are two checkboxes. The first one is the setting to include this material as a paper texture. The second is the option to use it as a brush tip shape. (You might remember the option used back in *Chapter 2*, *The Right Tools for the Job*, when we made a custom painting brush!) If you want any of these materials to also be available as a paper texture or brush tip while making custom tools, simply check the boxes next to these options.

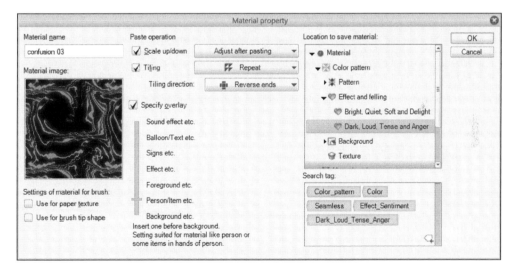

In the center of the **Material property** menu are options for repeating, scaling, and placement of the material. The first drop-down menu controls the scaling actions that occur with the material. The one currently selected for this material is that we'll scale and rotate it after it's pasted into our page.

The option **Expand in full** will take the material and expand it so that it is full size on the area without any repeating. This will ensure that you cover the entire canvas with your material and is useful on materials that you don't want to repeat or that aren't seamless.

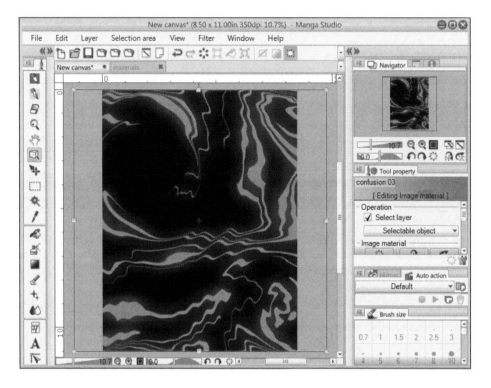

The **Fit to scale** option takes the material and sizes it to scale with your canvas area. As you can see in the following screenshot, the bounding box for the material matches with the edge of the canvas, and Manga Studio uses the tiling settings for the repeats on the top and bottom to fill the rest of the space.

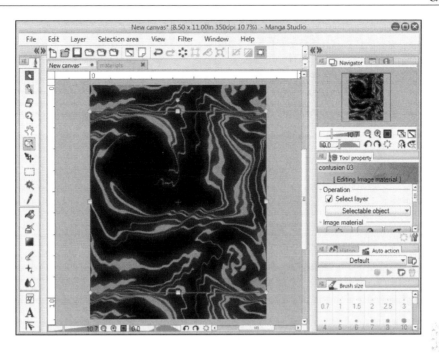

Adjust according to destination will size the material according to the pasting destination. Because the confusion material we've been using is square, we'll have to use a different material to see the differences between these two options. By making a long, skinny canvas in Manga Studio and then using the **Blurred Rainbow** material (which can be found under the **Image Material | Brush category**), we can best see the way that these options affect the material.

Fit to Scale on this material and this canvas adjusts the material to fit inside of the canvas, with white spaces around the edge because the material was sized so that the left and right edges will fit inside the image dimensions. The example beneath is the **Adjust according to destination** setting, which has made the top and bottom edges fit the canvas so that the material is covering the entire image.

The **Fit to Text** option will fit the material to the text on your page.

The next checkbox controls the **Tiling** settings for the material. Unchecking the box will turn tiling off, so that only one instance of the material will be used when pasting instead of creating a full covering over the canvas. Tiling is usually turned off for materials that you would only want one instance of, like dialog balloons and sound effects. But for seamless patterns like the **Confusion** background, we can change how the tiling works to create different looks.

This material is set to **Repeat** by default. Manga Studio will take the material and repeat it horizontally and vertically, all across the canvas. In the drop-down menu there are two other options—**Wrap** and **Flip**.

Wrap mirrors the material horizontally and vertically, depending on which side is being wrapped. Imagine that you are cutting down a cardboard box and you cut each of the folds on the side panels straight down to the bottom of the box, then laid them down. You would have a square in the center and then four side flaps, one coming from each side of the box. This is how Manga Studio interprets the material when this tiling option is used. As you can see in the following screenshot, it makes the **Confusion** background look a lot like a Rorschach test!

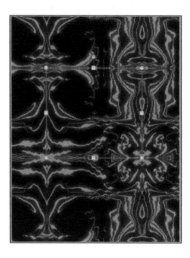

The **Flip** tiling option will reverse the material on the horizontal axis. Underneath the **Tiling** options is another drop-down for the direction in which the tiling will occur. Currently this pattern is set to **Reverse ends**, which means that it will continue to tile horizontally and vertically for the duration of the selected area. Changing this setting to **Horizontal Only** will make the material only repeat in the horizontal direction. **Vertical Only** will do just that—set it to tile only vertically!

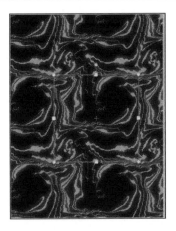

The next set of options is one that will be useful to understand so that we can save time later. This option is to specify to Manga Studio where you want the material to be pasted in the stack of layers. As you can see in the following screenshot, there's a checkbox to turn this option on and off, and then a slider bar to set where you wish to have this material land whenever you use it. Setting this correctly for how you intend to use a material will save you time because you won't have to drag a layer up or down every time that you use a pattern.

We're going to drag this particular material down to the **Background** level.

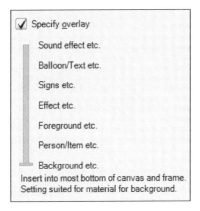

We always want to paste this on the bottom of the stack, underneath all our other elements. Click on **OK** and now, even if we have the topmost layer of our drawing selected, this material will paste at the bottom of the layers, just over the **Paper** level, every time that we use it.

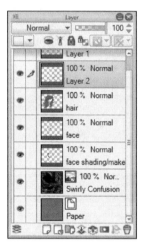

The right-most section of the **Material Property** window allows us to change our material's location and its tags. Right now we can see that our confusion material is showing under **Color pattern | Effect and Feeling | Dark, Loud | Tense and Anger.** Let's change it to the **Background** category. Click on the triangle next to **Background** and select **Artificial**.

Underneath the location you will see a list of the tags associated with this material. We're going to add a few of our own to make searching for this material easier. To add your own tags, click on the icon at the bottom of the tags window. A white text entry field will appear. Type in your new tag and then hit the *Enter* key on your keyboard. Keep doing this for any new tags that you wish to add to the material. Let's add the tags: **background, purple, swirl, feeling,** and **abstract**. Then click on the **OK** button to the right to save your changes.

Now if we go to our materials and search for background, look what happens!

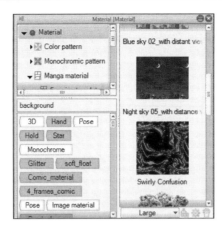

When we first searched on background, the confusion material didn't show as a result because it wasn't tagged with that search term. Now that we have it tagged as such, we can search for any of the tags that are associated and it will pull into the results. It requires an investment of time at first to go through and add any custom tags that you might need for your materials, but in the end it's worth it, for the time that you save not hunting for what you need later on.

One last thing on editing existing materials before we move on to making your own custom ones. What if you're working on a comic that's in black and white, but the material you want to use is in color? That's when we'll want to use the **Tonization** settings. Remember that information box that shows the material location when you first click on the thumbnail?

In the area that shows us the material name, type, and tags, there is a check box for **Tonization.** Once you click on this box, the **Settings...** button next to it will become active. Then click on the **Settings** button. This will open the **Simple tone settings,** where you can edit how Manga Studio will interpret the color of the material image to a grayscale screentone pattern.

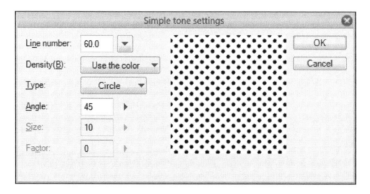

The higher the number under **Line Number**, the smaller the dots of the tone will be. The smaller the number, the larger the dots will be and they will therefore be more visible. The difference between 27.5 lines and 85 lines is the same principle as 72 dpi when compared to 300 dpi. More lines per inch equals smaller dots, and therefore a higher resolution (so to speak).

Density has two options: **Use the Color** and **Use the Brightness**. These affect how dense Manga Studio renders the dots depending on which option you use. Selecting **Use the Color** will, of course, have the program determine how dark and dense to put the screentone dots based on the darkness of the color of the material. **Use the Brightness** will base the density of dots on how bright the areas of the material are.

Type allows you to change the shape of the screentone dots. There are many different types, including everything from circles to diamonds to flowers, and even hearts. Since we're about to use a heart material, I think it would be cute to have the tone made of hearts, so that's what we'll select for this one.

Angle allows you to change the angle of the pattern of dots. It defaults to 45 degrees, but for our little heart tone we're going to change it to about 30 degrees. Click on the **OK** button.

For the fastest way to get our screentone right where we want it, use the *lasso* selection tool and trace around the outside of your figure so that the background is surrounded by the selection area. Once we paste in our material a layer mask will be formed so that it's only showing exactly where we wanted it to show — the insides of our selection — instead of on the entire canvas. This saves us a lot of time erasing out the extra bits of the image, and will allow us to continually manipulate the tone later if we need to move or resize it.

Now that we know how to edit the material that is already there, let's make some of our own!

Creating custom material

Now we're going to create several types of materials that will be unique to our projects. You can create materials from photos, textures, or elements that you've drawn in Manga Studio or in other graphics software.

Speech balloon

Let's start off by making a speech balloon. To do this, you can draw a shape that you would like to turn into a speech bubble. Maybe you have a villain character who needs a special type of "evil" balloon? You could try something like this for your shape!

This speech balloon was made just by stacking three ovals one on top of the other, two black and one red. Add some white or red text in it and it will look really sinister!

Make sure that your layers are flattened together before you register your material. If you've drawn a line art on one layer and then colored on another layer, merge the two layers together by using the keyboard shortcut *Ctrl + E* or by using the options under the **Layer** menu. If you don't merge your layers, the material will end up being only the layer that is currently active!

So, let's take our evil shape and make it into a word balloon material.

You'll notice that the evil text shape has just transparency on the outside. The black and red are both on the same layer so that we'll be saving them both at the same time with the material settings. We want the background of the image to be transparent because when we put this into a comic, we don't want a white box around the edge of our balloon.

Now that we have the balloon that we want to save to our material palette, we'll go to the **Edit** menu and click on **Register Image as material**.

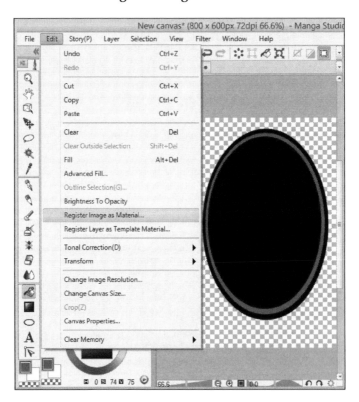

Once you click that you'll see a very familiar window again.

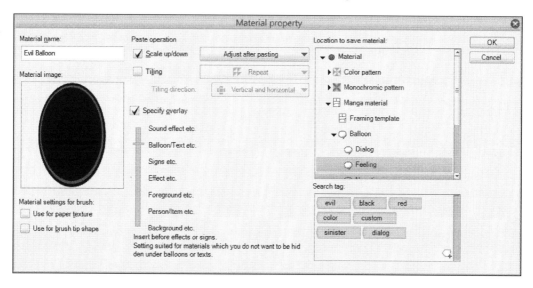

Let's enter a name for our new balloon. We don't want this material to tile, but we do want to specify the overlay. Make sure that it's set to **Balloon| Text.** Then we're going to store the material under **Manga Material | Balloon | Feeling.** I've added some tags to my balloon so that I can find it easily later using a keyword search. Once we're done, we'll hit **OK** and our new material settings will be saved.

Now we can use our new balloon behind text in our comic pages. Simply locate the image in the materials palette and paste it in, then add your text and you're done!

Getting splashy with sound effects

Sound effects are an important part of making a comic. If you find that you use a certain sound a lot, saving it as a material will save you from having to remake them over and over again.

Start with a blank canvas and use the text tool to type out your sound effect. Get creative, or you can do a search on the Internet for common sound effects used in Manga and comic books. You can find lists of them on websites, or make up your own. Let's do *Wa-boom!* for this example. Pick a font that you like for your chosen sound effect. The one I'm using for this example is called Damn Noisy Kids, and it came from www.1001fonts.com.

Let's put a stroke around our text. For my comic, I use white text with a black outline so that's what I'll use for this example. We'll be able to change the color on the fly later, so don't worry about that. Once you have your sound effect ready, right-click on the text layer in your **Layers** palette and **Rasterize Layer**.

Using the **Magic Wand** tool, we will click on the transparent parts of our layer, outside the text. To make the outside stroke we need to reverse the selection. Under the **Select** menu, click on the **Reverse Selection** option. Now the outline of the text will be selected, as shown in the following screenshot:

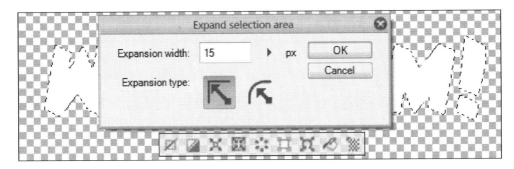

Next we'll expand the selection area. It may take some experimenting to get the width that you want. I settled on 15 pixels eventually. Now we'll make a new layer underneath the text layer. Select black as your foreground color and fill the selection.

Now use *Shift + Ctrl + E* to merge both of your layers. Now we're going to add some dimension to our sound effect. Under the **Edit** Menu, go to **Transform | Mesh Transform**. A grid of edit points will appear over the text. Here's where you can get creative with your sound effect shape. Since this is an explosion sound, let's make the middle bulge out and the ends angle a bit so the word looks like it's exploding out.

Once you have your text transformed, use **Register image as Material** under the **Edit** Menu. Make sure to set your tags so that you can find your material later!

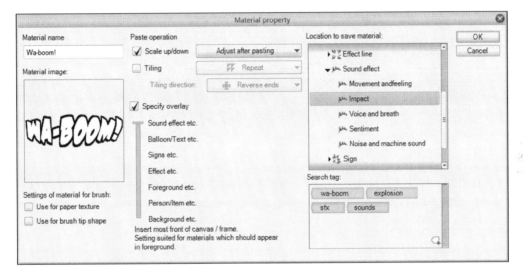

Now we have a base black and white sound effect. But what if we want to color the letters when we use it? There's a ton of ways that you could add color to the letters, but here's two that are really easy to do.

First, paste the sound effect into your canvas from the **Materials** palette. For the first coloring method we're going to add our color to a layer underneath the text. Set your **Materials** layer to the **Multiply** blending mode. Then create a layer beneath it and add a gradient or fill the layer with color.

The **Multiply** blending mode turns white pixels transparent, and keeps black pixels opaque. At least, that's a very simple explanation of it! So now when we put color (or anything else, including other materials) on another layer, the letters will appear to be see-through.

You can also add color above the sound effect too using a clipping mask! To do this, put a layer above the sound effect layer. Right-click on the empty layer and select the **Clip at layer below** option under the **Layer settings** menu. This will take the pixels of the layer directly below this layer and mask it out, making the outlines of both layers match.

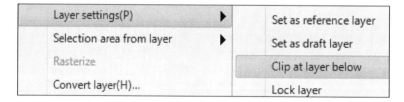

Now add a fill or a gradient to the top layer. Set the top layer to **Multiply** so that the material beneath it will be visible. As you can see on the image below, the gradient is filling the entire layer but we can only see the parts of it that cross the layer below. With the gradient set to **Multiply**, the black outline of the sound effect still looks black and the white sections look colored. Now we can infinitely change the color layer to anything we wish without affecting the material itself.

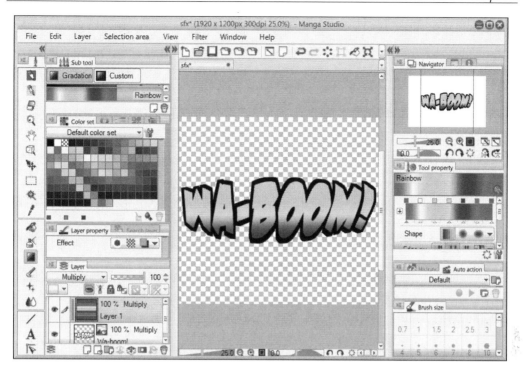

The following examples were all done by changing the top layer in this method. The flames on the third image are another Manga Studio material laid over the top of the sound effect and then clipped to the layer below and set to **Multiply**.

Making plaids

Plaid is one of those clothing patterns that you see everywhere, and it looks hard to draw! But it's really not, once you have the basics down. And if you create a pattern and then register it as a material, you can reuse it again and again. A definite time-saver if your comic is about schoolgirls in plaid skirts, right? In this section I'm going to walk you through the creation of a simple repeating pattern. It's just a grid, so don't let it intimidate you! You can do this, just follow along! You'll be a master of plaid in no time!

The first thing that we need to do is make a new canvas. We're going to make a square. I went with 6 inches by 6 inches and 300 dpi. You could make your pattern smaller than that, it's always better though to scale down instead of up, so keep that in mind. If you'll be doing large 300-600 dpi drawings for print, you don't want to have to scale a 72 dpi material up to fit.

We can also leave the **Paper Color** option unchecked and start off with a transparent canvas.

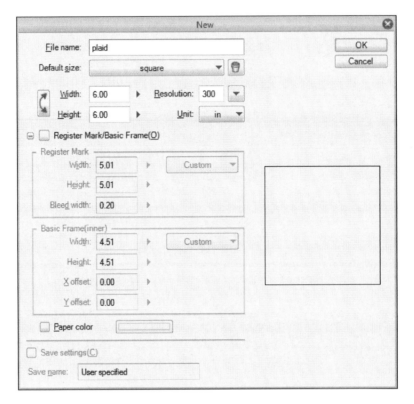

The first thing that we'll do once we have our square canvas is lay a grid over the top of it. Go to **View | Grid** and Manga Studio will automatically show a grid for you. Then we'll fill in our base layer with the color of our choice. Let's make a soft blue, purple, and pink plaid for now. Pick your base color and then press *Alt + Del* to fill, or go to **Edit | Fill.** (You can also use the paint bucket tool if you would like.)

Next we'll put a contrasting color stripe down the center of our canvas. Count the squares on your grid, and then make a stripe of purple on a new layer. My grid is six-by-six large squares, so I made a 3 square wide stripe and set it so that there was a square and a half on either side of the edges.

Make another new layer. Now we're going to use the line tool and a dark blue to draw vertical lines in the center of each of our light blue areas, and every two large squares of the grid. We also will need a line at the top and the bottom of the square, but you need to make sure that you only use half the width of your brush there! Since the pattern will be repeating at the top and bottom we don't want the lines there to show up as double the width of all the other lines.

[Turn on **Snap to Grid** under **View** or by using *Ctrl + 3* on your keyboard. This will make keeping your lines perfectly aligned to your grid much easier.]

How wide you make your line tool here is really up to you. My setting for the dark blue line was 35 on the line tool in Manga Studio. You can make your lines thinner or thicker, if you desire.

For the next step we're going to adjust our line width to slightly smaller and add more lines to our design. Using a line width of 25 and a light pink color, add a horizontal line on each large square grid mark between the dark blue lines. For the last step, take white and make vertical lines—one in the exact center of the design, and one in the center of each light blue area. If you have **Snap to Grid** turned on, you'll need to turn it off for this part, as each of the light blue areas is three small squares wide so the vertical lines will need to go in the center of the second square to be aligned correctly.

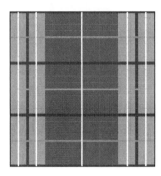

Drawing out your initial plaid pattern on individual layers makes it easier for you to make other variations later. Simply select a layer and change the color of the lines and you'll have a new look in a matter of seconds—no redrawing required!

Save your file before we continue, either as a Manga Studio (`.lip`) or Photoshop (`.psd`) file. You should make it a habit to save your custom material files in these formats because it will be easier to go back and make changes later should you need to edit or fix something. Or, like in the tip above, if you decided that you wanted your plaid to be green and red instead, you could go back to the source file and change the individual layers to suit your new needs, rather than redrawing the entire pattern.

Now that you have your file saved, we're going to flatten the image so that it's all one layer. *Ctrl + Shift + E* combines all the visible layers of your image, or you can navigate to **Layer | Combine Visible Layers**. Then we're going to register our image as a material, which can be found under the **Edit** menu. This will bring up the **Material Property** window that we spent a lot of time working with at the beginning of the chapter.

Give your material a name such as `Blue and Purple Plaid`, something that is descriptive so you can identify it later. Turn both the **Scale up/down** option on and the **Tiling** option as well. **Scale up/down** we're going to set to **Adjust after pasting**. This way we can scale the material to fit the scale of our image after we've put it on our canvas.

For the Material location, choose **Color pattern | Pattern | Clothes pattern**. Then we'll want to add some tags so we can find our material later on. Some suggested tags are: **plaid, clothing, clothes, blue, purple, custom, pattern**, and **seamless**.

Now we can use our custom pattern! Let's draw a skirt and add our material to see how the pattern looks.

Looking good! Though I'm going to share with you a little tip to make your plaid look more convincing and less like a flat pattern that we threw on here. It takes a bit of extra time but it's going to make your results look all the better. It can really sell the realism of your illustration on closer shots too.

We're going to break this skirt down in to three parts. The first part will be the waistband area above the pleats. The second part will be the pleats on the left side of the drawing, and the third part will be the two right-most pleats that are being blown by the wind.

First step, let's use the lasso selection tool to select the top part of our skirt. Don't be fussy about the edges – in fact, go outside of the lines some! We'll need the extra space for a transformation that we'll be doing in the next step. Then we'll paste our material into our canvas. Because we have an active selection, the plaid pattern will be masked to our selection. Resize your material as desired.

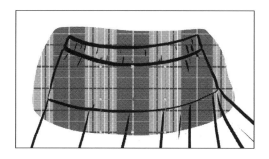

Next we need to do a little adjusting on our plaid material to make it look more like it's actually curving around this form. Because let's face it, real fabric would follow the contours of a body! So we need to make this look more like it's really a skirt instead of a drawing of a skirt with a texture pasted onto it.

To make this edit, we'll be using the **Mesh Transform** tool. But before we can use it we have to rasterize our materials layer first. Right-click on your material and select the **Apply Mask to Layer** option. This will combine the layer mask that was applied to the material from our initial selection to the material. Then right-click again and select **Rasterize Layer**.

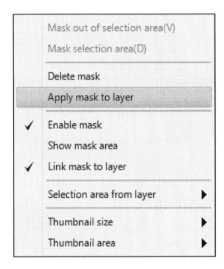

Now we are ready to use the mesh transform tool! Under the **Edit** menu, go to **Transform | Mesh Transformation**. A grid of editable points will appear over your material area. Pull and push the points around to make the lines of the plaid better match the lines of your skirt.

You may have to do some experimenting to get it right, but the mesh transform is one of the best tools in all of Manga Studio.

Once you have the lines of your plaid curving in a way that matches your line art, hit *Enter* to apply the transformation. Then take an eraser or make a Layer Mask and clean up your edges.

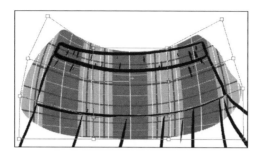

Next you'll do the same thing to the remaining sections of your clothing. Since the two right pleats are going in a different direction from the rest of the pleats, we're going to break the skirt into two sections. Use the lasso tool around your skirt, paste the material on, scale and rotate the pattern to match up with your other sections, and then mesh transform. Once you're done, you should have something like this:

Now it's time to add some shading and highlights to make our skirt look even more like a skirt! I made two layers above the patterns—one set to **Multiply** blending mode with an opacity of 80 percent for the shadows. Then the highlights were created on another layer using a light blue color and a soft brush. The **Highlight** layer is set to **Normal** for the blending mode but it's also at 70 percent opacity to let the pattern show through.

Finishing an image with materials

To wrap this chapter up, I thought I would show the process of creating an illustration using as many different materials as I could. The first step, of course, was to come up with the pose and make a sketch. I used the custom sketching pencil that we made back in *Chapter 2, The Right Tools for the Job*. The canvas that was used is 11 inches by 8.5 inches and 350 dpi.

The sketch layer was then changed to a draft layer so that the lines turn blue. The custom Ink brush—also discussed in *Chapter 2, The Right Tools for the Job*, was then used on another layer to finalize the lines.

Time to add color!

Now for materials on the clothing. The T-shirt design, the lace on the armbands, and the plaid on the skirt are all custom-made materials. In fact, the plaid design is the same plaid from the last section, just edited for different colors!

Using a material for something like a T-shirt design can be a life saver. Rather than having to redraw the design on your character in every panel, you can simply use the material, rasterize it, and then edit it to fit the curve of the shirt. Use the **Free Transform** and **Mesh Transform** tools to adjust your material and it will look like it was drawn over again without you having to spend the time drawing it more than once!

Finally we'll finish up with a photo material for a background. The photo has had two adjustment layers placed over the top of it to change the color and make it blend more with the character. The splatters are from the Manga Studio 5 material library. Even my signature at the bottom of the drawing and the website address are a custom material!

Summary

I hope that this chapter has shown you some of the many ways that materials are useful and can help you create your comics even faster than before. Let's recap on what we've learned and then move on to the next chapter, shall we? We covered:

- How to navigate and search materials
- How to use materials in a scene
- How to edit material, including tags, insert points, and categories
- How to make custom materials

We're going to hit the third dimension with the next chapter. Let's get started!

6
It's Only a (3D) Model

3D models are present in the **Materials** section of Manga Studio. However, working with 3D models is so different from working with a 2D pattern that giving them their own chapters only seemed right. Having 3D models of figures and other objects available right in Manga Studio is a really useful thing! It makes getting reference for a difficult pose much easier. You don't have to scour the Internet, or get friends together for a photo shoot when you're on a deadline.

A good thing to remember though about using 3D elements in your work is that you should really use them as a reference, a jumping off point, instead of the be-all-and-end-all of the piece. Use a model to get the general pose that you want, then draw off of it. You really shouldn't throw a 3D model in with 2D artwork and leave it. It takes more work to make the combination of things looks good than is usually worth it. Most of the time 2D art with 3D elements stuck in just look awkward and strange. So if you can, try not to do it. Just don't. Trust me on this one.

In this chapter we're going to cover these exciting topics:

- Inserting a 3D model into your canvas
- Using pre-posed models
- Altering model proportions
- Moving the 3D camera
- Creating a custom pose and saving it
- Importing 3D models

Now let's get started going into the third dimension!

Inserting and positioning models in your canvas

So the first thing we'll need to do is make a blank canvas. I'm using my generic 8.5 inch by 11 inch setting at 350 dpi for the examples in this chapter. Then open your **Materials** palette, either by clicking on the double arrows to open it if you have it docked in your workspace, or going to **Window | Material | Material [3D]** to pull up the palette.

Manga Studio will load all of the 3D materials since we're in the **3D** category. For now, let's just choose any old model to work with. I'm going to use the **Draw up** model because it's a basic pose so it will be easy to work with.

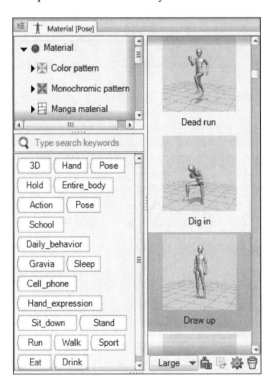

You can search for and edit the 3D model materials in much the same way as we searched for and edited them in *Chapter 5, Living in a Material World*. Manga Studio does not allow you to select 3D models for brush tip shapes or paper textures, and you cannot change the paste location, scale operation, or tiling. However, you can edit the location that the model is saved in, and edit the tags just as we did with 2D materials.

Click on **Paste a selected material** on the canvas icon to insert your model into your blank canvas. Since we're only going to be working with the one model right now, either collapse or close the **Materials** palette to get it out of your way.

Now we have our model on our canvas and we can get down to the nitty-gritty of working with it!

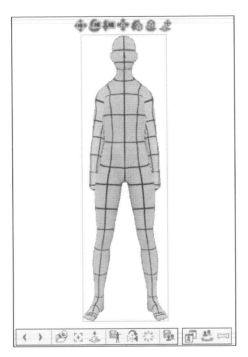

At first glance, there's a lot of stuff going on here and it might be a bit scary. But trust me when I say that it's really not! Let's go through everything one item at a time and you'll see what I mean.

First, let's start off with the bar of icons that are over our model's head. The first three of these icons control the position and rotation of our virtual camera. The last four icons control the position and rotation of our model.

Controlling the 3D camera

Let's talk about the camera first. When you work in 3D, you usually have three elements that you're working with—a model, a camera, and a ground plane. Think of the ground plane as the floor of your virtual room—except that in 3D space you can put things above or below the ground plane. The ground plane is there for reference when you're positioning your model or your camera, and it makes it much easier to line multiple models up in perspective. We can only see the ground plane when we are moving the model.

1. **Camera Horizontal and Vertical Control**

2. **Camera Rotation Control**

3. **Camera Zoom Control**

4. **Model Horizontal and Vertical Control**

5. **Model Vertical Rotation Control**

6. **Model Horizontal Rotation Control**

7. **Model Z-axis to Camera Control**

Left-click and hold down the mouse button on the **Camera Horizontal and Vertical Control** icon above your character's head. Then drag your mouse around and see what happens.

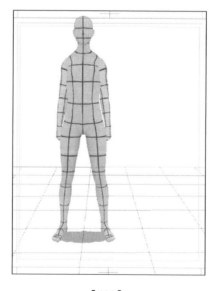

The grid beneath the character's feet is the ground plane. The first icon in our top bar is in charge of the horizontal and vertical orientation of our camera, so as you drag the model it will move around your canvas in the X and Y axis, depending on how you move your mouse (or tablet stylus, touch pad, or whatever you're using to manipulate your model. Personally I find this type of operation to be better suited to a mouse than a tablet pen).

Alright, so the first icon on the menu controls our camera's horizontal and vertical position. The second icon has a camera and some curved arrows—it controls the rotation of your camera. Left-click and drag around. Just for fun, let's drag toward the top of the canvas so that we go underneath the model.

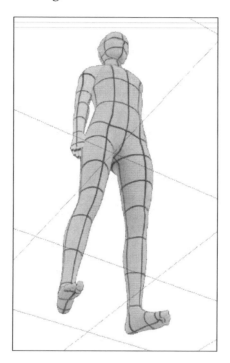

As you can see from the preceding screenshot, our ground plane hasn't moved, but the camera has moved so that it's underneath the ground plane. Remember at this point that we're not moving the model, instead we're moving our own viewpoint of the model. Think of it like being in life-drawing class and moving your seat so that you get a different angle on your subject, instead of making the subject move for you.

There's just one more axis that we can control for our camera, and that's how close or far away it is to our model. Left-click and drag on the third camera control icon to zoom in and out on your model. Dragging up will move the camera further away, dragging down will move it closer. Seems a bit backward at first, if you ask me, but you get used to it after just a little bit.

Now, by using those three camera controls you can get just about any shot that you want on this model! Let's zoom in for a really dramatic angle of our character looking up toward some off-screen danger!

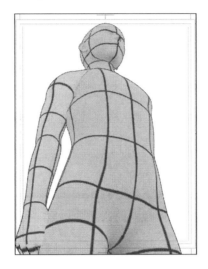

Now that we have the camera positioned the way that we want, we can use the model as a basis for our drawing. What I like to do is take the opacity of the model layer down to about 50 percent in the Layers window and then sketch over the top of it. An example of a way that you could use this pose and camera angle is as follows:

In addition to being able to position the camera manually, you can also use the pre-set camera angles that Manga Studio provides. These cover some of the more common camera angles and can be used for a wide variety of uses. To illustrate the camera angles, I'm going to use one of the 3D character models instead of just the pose model. The character models can be found under **Materials | 3D | Character**. They are a male and a female "doll" with clothes, facial expressions, hair, and accessories that can be set just as the posing models can be. We'll talk a little bit more about the characters in a minute, for now though let's switch up camera angles using the pre-sets.

First, place a character or a pose model onto your canvas. Then look at the bottom editing bar. You'll see an icon that looks like a folder with a camera coming out of it. This is the **Specify camera** angle from pre-set icon.

Click on the icon and a grid with drawings of the different angles will come up. The angle that we currently have selected is highlighted blue and has a little checkmark in the corner. Since we haven't done anything to the camera, we're on the very basic, straight on camera angle by default.

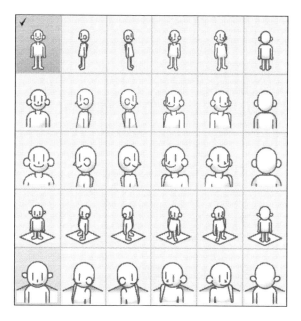

Let's select one of the angles on the bottom row. In fact, I like the fourth one from the left, the one with the right ear toward the camera. We click on the icon of our desired camera angle, and Manga Studio will immediately move the camera to that position.

Using the pre-set camera angles along with moving the camera manually will allow you to always get the reference shot that you need for your work.

Positioning the model

The right-most four icons on the top bar of our 3D model control the position of the model itself or of a selected surface of the model.

1. **Camera Horizontal and Vertical Control**
2. **Camera Rotation Control**
3. **Camera Zoom Control**
4. **Model Horizontal and Vertical Control**
5. **Model Vertical Rotation Control**
6. **Model Horizontal Rotation Control**
7. **Model Z-axis to Camera Control**

Remember a minute ago when we talked about the ground plane and how when we moved the camera, the model and the ground stayed the same in relationship to one another? Well, look what happens when we move the actual model down using **Model Horizontal and Vertical Control**.

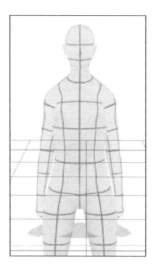

The shadow on the ground plane that should be under the model's feet is now up around the thighs, because we've moved the model down into the ground plane. In essence, the model is now half trapped in the floor.

Now that the character is closer to the ground plane, we can make her lay down on it by adjusting this rotation so that she's on her back, facing up toward the top of our canvas. The **Model Horizontal Control** will allow us to further customize our character's positioning. Let's rotate the character so that she's laying on her side on the ground plane, facing toward us. It will take some adjusting at first but you'll get better at manipulating the model with some practice.

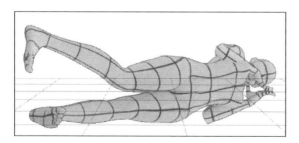

So by now you may be wondering why in the world there are controls for both moving the camera and the model around. Because aside from the position of the ground plane, there's not too much difference between moving the actual model and moving our virtual camera, right? Well, if you're just working with character models, you're right. There's just about no difference. However, when you start to include other models in your setup, that's when things like camera position and the position of the character start to get important. To see what I mean, let's add a desk chair to our scene.

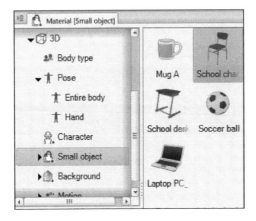

In the **Small Object** category of our 3D materials, you'll find several models. Select the school chair and add it to your canvas. Use the seventh icon on your top editing bar to move the chair back behind your character if it's not already there. This last icon manipulates the position of your model in 3D space, moving it both closer to and further from the camera as well as up and down from the ground plane.

Okay, get your chair positioned somewhere! Got it? Now go back to your camera rotation control and drag around.

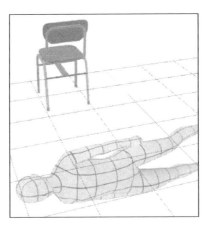

As you can see in the preceding screenshot, the camera rotates around both models at the same time when we adjust its position. So now the relationship between our models and the ground plane is important, because we have multiple elements in the scene that we're working around. So keep these things in mind when you're working with your camera and your models. Setting up your scene correctly from the start will save you a lot of headache in the end.

Using the character models

In the **3D | Character** category are two models, a school girl character and a school boy character. When you add one to your canvas it will appear in a default pose—which is standing straight up with arms out at the sides. If you wish to use a **Character** model with one of the pre-set poses, it's really easy to do. Simply find the pose that you want in the **Pose** category, then click on the thumbnail in the **Materials** palette and drag the pose to the **Character** model. Once you let go, the character will be repositioned.

A neat thing about the character models though is that you can change their hair, expressions, and clothes too. So if you're having trouble getting that sad, teary eyed expression on your character, the character models could be a quick and easy reference to help you out.

On the bottom editing bar you'll see five icons that weren't there when we were using just the pose model. The icon with the smiley face is what you'll click to change your character's expression. Experiment with the different options to get a feel for what each one looks like!

The icon that shows the top of a head, and some hair, is the controls for the hair. There are several pre-set hairstyles that you can choose for both the male and female character models. The default female model has bangs and ponytails that are also available in the accessories tab.

At the time of this writing, there is no way to change the character eye or hair color. However, the Manga Studio Official User Guide shows characters with many more hairstyles and colors in the 3D section, so additional content may be forthcoming.

Click on some of the hairstyles just to get a feel for what they look like on the model. If you have trouble drawing a certain type of hair they might be good as a starting off point at least for reference.

The **Body** icon gives you choices for different outfits, which on the default characters are three school uniforms and a set of casual clothes just to get you started. You can select one of these and it will be applied to the model automatically.

Let's say that we're writing a young girl's comic (referred to as *Shoujo* in Japanese Manga), and we have a frame where the main female protagonist meets the handsome young male protagonist. They meet because she kicks a soccer ball and it hits him and knocks him over. She comes over to him and offers him a hand up, apologizing for the fact that she hit the young man. Soon they will fall in love and it affects the rest of the comic.

Here's what our reference image made with our character models might look like. Both of these poses are from the pre-set models—the only one that has been altered is the girl's, and that was only to stick her right arm out a little bit further to see her hand at this angle. (The pose for the girl is the **Pass Out Papers** pose)

Then the comic frame that we draw from the reference might look something like this!

Striking a pose

So now we know how to navigate around with our camera and to reposition a pre-posed model, how can we make custom poses? Manga Studio won't constrain you to using just the poses that have been included in the **Materials** palette! You can edit the position of the model easily, using the same icons that we just discussed in the last section. Let's do some practice right now so you can see how it works.

First, we'll need some pose inspiration. I love to draw action, so I'm taking inspiration from martial arts moves. If you need to, sketch out a simple gesture drawing of the pose that you have in mind.

Next up we're going to choose one of the pre-positioned models that is close to our desired custom pose. Which base model you choose is really up to you. Let's go with **Rise to full height** because the legs are already spread fairly far apart, just like in our gesture drawing.

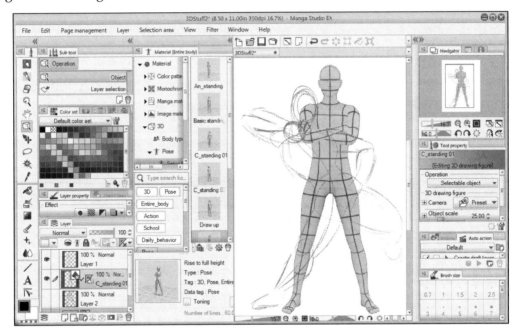

You can work with your gesture drawing layer either above or below your 3D model. Personally, I like having the sketch above the model because it makes for easier reference. Do what feels most comfortable to you though!

Okay, first thing's first, let's get the spine of our 3D model to match up a bit better with our gesture. Our hips need to go toward the right and twist some, and the shoulders need to come toward the left so we get a curve in the spine.

 Remember that in drawing, the line of action is the most important thing, and that line usually runs down the spine. Getting the spine in the correct position off the bat will make it much easier to get your pose details down.

Hover your mouse cursor over the pelvis of your character model. After a moment the pelvis area will highlight red. This is to show you the section of your model that you're about to select. Left-click on the hips and they will remain highlighted. Also, a sphere made of red, green, and blue lines will appear around the hips. This is how you control the rotation of the joint that you have selected. Hover over one of the lines until it turns yellow. Then left-click and drag your mouse.

When you rotate the hips, your entire model is going to rotate. The hips are a fixed control point, so they're essentially locked. So we'll rotate our hips so that the right-hand side is up higher than the left-hand side, just how we have it in our sketch. Now we'll have to do some more moving of the torso, but let's get the legs in relative position first.

Hover over the top of the thigh, just below the hip, and click to select your joint. Then use the rotation tools to space the legs further apart. If you look carefully you will also see a yellow box by your joint when you've selected it. You can use this to drag the joint to position it—that's a faster way but it's less precise, so experiment with both methods to see which one you prefer. Personally, I like to use the rotation controls because it just feels like I have a better handle on those than on the box control.

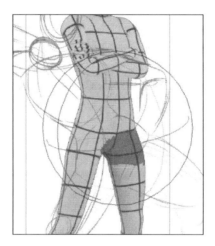

 You may need to rotate or move the virtual camera to see the controls.

Remember as you're rotating your joint that the different colored lines on your control sphere each rotate on a different axis. You can tell which line does which direction based on the way that it's pointing. For instance, if you look at the preceding screenshot, you'll see that the red control goes from left to right, horizontal across the canvas. So if we hover on that control and drag our mouse, that's the direction we're going to rotate our selected joint. We want to bend this leg further out to the side of the model, as we sketched out in our gesture. So we'll use the blue control line because it's going up and down on the side of the model.

Once we have our legs positioned just about how we want them, we can work on the torso. The torso has three editable areas, which I like to call the **Waist**, **Upper Abs**, and the **Ribcage**. The **Ribcage** area is the largest control of the torso, going from the shoulders down to the bottom of the ribs. The other two sections are between the bottom of the ribcage and the pelvis.

Click on the **Waist** area and rotate it to the side, trying to match the curve of our sketch as closely as possible. Do the same with the **Upper Abs** and the **Ribcage** areas, curving them. You might need to move the arms out of the way if you chose a pose that had them in front of the body. Look at the following screenshot and you'll note that I had to move the arms far out away from the chest to position the torso.

Let's get the feet and legs exactly how we want them before we work on the upper part of the body. We need to rotate the right leg (our left) out some to get the knee position and the foot to match our sketch. Select the top of the thigh and move it so that the knee faces out, then do the same for the foot until they better match the gesture drawing.

We need to bend the knee on the left leg (our right) to match our sketch. Select the area directly below the knee and a sphere with only one color line will appear. This is because knees only bend in one direction, so this joint is constrained to that bend! Rotate the knee so that the leg is bent, then select the foot and move it to match the sketch as well.

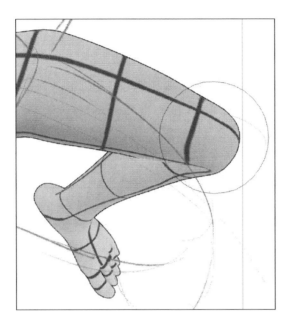

The thigh in the preceding screenshot was rotated too far to the outside, so I actually pulled it back in some more. Once you have practiced using the 3D features of Manga Studio, it will become much easier and faster to make the edits on these models.

Once you're happy with the position of your legs, let's go ahead and get that head the way that we want it. Select the head and rotate it so that it's facing towards the right. You'll probably have to select the neck and do the same thing to get it as far rotated as we've suggested in our gesture sketch.

 You can also easily rotate a part by selecting it and then using the scroll wheel on your mouse.

So far, here's how our pose looks.

Getting there! Now we just have the arms and hands to move and then we can use our pose for a drawing. The right arm (the one that's the left arm of the character) is probably going to be the most difficult to get into position, so let's work on it first.

Thank goodness that the creators of Manga Studio realized what a pain positioning fingers was going to be and they gave us a tool to make it easier. The first time I wrote this chapter, I didn't know about this tool, so I moved all the fingers the hard way and selected each individual joint! Take my advice, don't do it the hard way unless that's the way that you really prefer to do it!

Locate your **Tool Property** window, you may have to go to **Window | Tool Property** to bring it up if it's been closed. With your 3D model selected, click on the icon with the two wrenches on it in the lower right corner.

This will bring up additional options. Make sure that you have one of the hands selected of your model. Then go to the **Pose** menu in the **Tool Property** window.

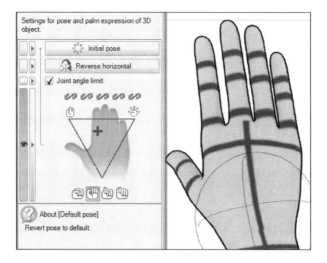

The top button in this menu will reset our model to the initial pose (the pose with the feet together and both arms out at the sides). The next one down will reverse the pose horizontally. But what we really want is that hand with the triangle over it and the funny symbols above the fingers. Because that is our hand control, and it makes adjusting the fingers so easy!

The further to the left that you move the crosshairs, the closer together the fingers become. The further to the right, and the further away they become. The top of the triangle is how open the fingers are, and the bottom point of the triangle is how closed they are. And at the bottom of that window are four pre-set fist poses that can be initialized with the click of the mouse.

Those strange looking "S" symbols at the tops of the fingers are actually locks for each individual finger. So, say that we wanted to make a peace sign hand gesture.

First we'll click on the closed fist pre-set gesture so that we close all our fingers down to the palm. Then click on the locks above the thumb, ring, and pinkie fingers and drag the crosshairs up so that the pointer and middle fingers are open and spread apart. Instant peace sign with just a few mouse clicks!

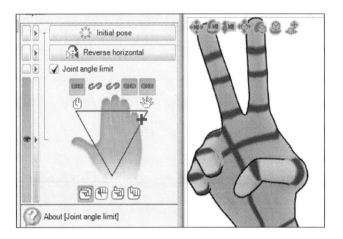

Though since the pose we're going for has closed fists, we'll go back to that pre-set after unlocking all the fingers. Now that we have our hand ready to go, we can position the rest of the arm. There are two controls for the shoulders that can help get the arm bent out to the side the way that we've positioned it in our sketch. Use those and the elbow control and make adjustments until you're satisfied with the way the arm looks.

Once you have one arm and hand in the pose that you want them to be in, it's time to do the same to the other arm. I like to position the hand first and then put the arm in place.

With the second arm in place, we're done posing our model! Here's how it turned out.

Now, if we wanted to save this pose so we can use it over again, there's a way to do that on the lower editing bar that shows up under your model's feet. This little icon serves the purpose:

It is the **Register pose to Materials palette** command. Click on it, and our familiar Material property window will appear. Let's name our pose `Martial Arts 01`. Store it in the **3D-Pose-Entire Body** category and add some tags. Some suggested tags are: **martial arts, full body, fist, kick, action**, and **custom**.

Now when we go into our **Entire Body** category, **Martial Arts 01** shows up as an option in our menu, and we can use the pose over and over again.

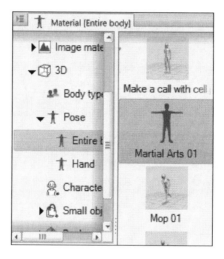

And now you can use your posed model for reference for your character.

Altering proportions

So now that you know how to manipulate the individual bits of the pose and character models, what happens if you need a reference for a character whose body type doesn't fit the standard? Maybe it's a child character, or a really skinny one. There are three different controls for the proportions of your model, so worry not!

Start off with a pose model in a blank canvas. The one pictured here is the **Well, Well** pose. Now take a look at the bottom editing bar under your model's feet. The three icons on the right are the ones that we'll be focusing on for this section.

The first icon, the one that looks like two pictures of a person stacked on top of each other, is for quick editing. The middle icon let's us get a little bit more in depth, and the third icon is very in-depth! Lets take a look at the simple commands first. Click on the first icon and this screen will come up.

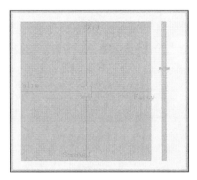

The slider on the right dictates the height of the model. Dragging the rectangle further down will make the model shorter, and dragging it up will make it taller of course. The quadrants mark off different pre-set proportions that you can mix by dragging the square in the center out. So let's say that we want to make a character who is a short, slim child. We'll drag the height control down and then take the box in the center of our quadrants and pull it up and to the left, towards the **Kid** and **Slim** labels.

Likewise, if we want to make a pudgy child character, we would move the cursor toward the right instead of toward the **Slim** section of the graph. If you're looking to just make quick proportion adjustments, this tool is the way to go. But if you're wanting to make a more comprehensive mix of the four traits that Manga Studio uses, then you'll need the next icon over on our editing bar.

This icon brings up the more detailed body shape and size settings. There are four sliders, each labeled with the traits, and you can mix all of them however you'd like to.

Dragging the slider to the right will add more of a trait, and to the left will take more of that trait away. Having them all set to **0** will give us the default model proportions.

And, if you need even more control over the parts of your model, well that's when you want our final icon in this section of the editing bar. This menu gives us complete control over the length and width of every part of the model, from the head down to the feet. Just for fun, let's take the arm length and the leg length all the way up.

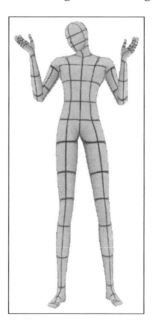

The hands, feet, torso, and head all stayed the same, but now the legs and arms are very long. You can use tricks like this to get the proportions for hulking characters, or maybe humanoid monsters with spindly limbs. Or even for tiny characters, say if your comics have dwarves or halflings because you're writing a fantasy story. The model in the next example has short arm length, leg length, and torso length, but large hands and feet.

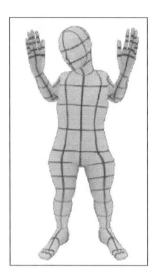

When you change the model proportions, you can still change to any of the pre-set poses simply by finding the one that you want in the **Materials** window, then clicking and dragging it to the model that you wish to repose. You can even use the custom poses that you've saved to the materials as well. Remember **Martial Arts 01** that we created earlier in the chapter? Here's our short character in that saved pose.

Of course, since we changed up the limb lengths, there's strangeness going on with the left arm. But a quick rotation of the shoulder would fix that and we'd be ready to go ahead with the drawing.

When you have proportions that you like and want to save, you can register them to your Materials palette for quick reuse later on. Click on the **Register 3D** drawing to material palette icon, to the left of the icons that you used to adjust your body proportions. Let's save this little character first, okay? Click on the icon, then give it a name, something that you'll remember later. We'll save this in the **3D-Body Type** category. Add any tags that you'd like and then click on the **OK** button.

When we go under our **Body Type** category in the materials layer, our **Dwarf Character** body type is there and ready to use over and over again.

Importing models

Custom models can be imported into Manga Studio 5, so long as they are a C2FR, FBX, LWO, LWS, OBJ, 6KT, or 6KH file format. If you download a model from the Internet and it's in a .zip file, you may need to unzip the model in order to import it. Some models can be dragged in directly from the .zip file. However, if the model doesn't import from the ZIP file, try extracting the files and importing them again.

Importing a model into Manga Studio is as simple as a drag-and-drop. On your computer, locate the file where your custom model is located. Then simply left-click and drag the file onto your Manga Studio canvas. I have a model of a horse that I want to import to this page, for example:

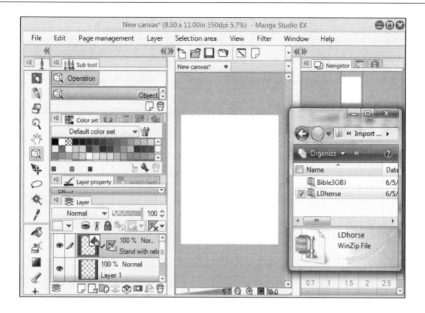

When you release your mouse button, the model will be imported into your canvas. Now I have a horse model to rotate around and work into my scene.

 If your imported model is too large or too small for the rest of your scene, go to the **Tool Property** menu. There is an option there to adjust the **Object Scale**, and it defaults to **25**. Adjusting this number up and down will make your model larger or smaller. In this case, the horse model was far too large for the scene, so I pulled it down to **4.5** in scale. Then the female drawing doll was increased to **30** on scale so that she wouldn't be too small next to the horse.

Here's our horse model being lead by our **Female** drawing doll. You can get creative with some of the pre-set poses, by the way. The model above is in the 'open a door' pose, and the only change I've made is to close the hands so that in the final drawing she'll be holding a rope.

 Imported models cannot be saved to the **Materials** palette, so you must import them separately for each new project that you want to use them in.

Summary

Phew! I know that we've covered a lot this chapter. But I hope that now you know just how useful these 3D models can be in assisting you with difficult angles and getting proportions accurate on your characters. I hope that by using these tools you'll become a more confident, and competent, artist.

To review, here's what we learned this chapter.

- Inserting models into the Manga Studio canvas
- Moving the virtual camera and the 3D model
- Using and editing character models
- Posing the drawing dolls
- Saving custom poses
- Changing model proportions
- Importing custom models

Are you ready for some action now? Because that's what we're getting into, in the next chapter!

7
Ready! Set! Action!

It's time to talk about Action! And I don't mean drawing fight scenes in your comics. I mean **Auto actions**, which are some of the best things you could ever learn how to use if you want to really streamline your processes and save some time doing repetitive functions.

So what is an Auto action? It's a saved set of steps that Manga Studio can play back, with the click of the mouse or the press of a keyboard key. Auto actions can do any number of things, from setting up files with layers, to changing the resolution of pages, and saving them for the Web. Have you ever had to open up a bunch of images and resize all of them, one at a time, going through the steps manually? Auto actions take away the monotonous part and play back the steps that have been recorded in them instantly.

Here's what we'll talk about in this chapter:

- Using actions
- Action sets
- Recording custom actions
- Playing part of an action
- Keyboard shortcut assignments for commonly used actions
- Importing and exporting

Using existing actions

Before we get into the nitty-gritty of making our own actions, let's take a look at the ones that have already been included with Manga Studio so that you get a feel for how they work. To get started, pull up your Actions palette by navigating to **Window | Auto action**. You will see a screen as shown in the following screenshot:

The first two actions create new layers. Let's use the first one to make a layer to sketch on. Highlight the **Create draft layer** action in the **Auto action** palette. At the bottom of the palette, click on the triangle icon. This plays the steps of the selected action.

When we click on the this icon, the action automatically completes itself. If you have your Layers palette open you will see a layer named **draft** now in it as shown in the following screenshot. We can do sketching on this layer and it won't be visible when we export to file formats such as JPG.

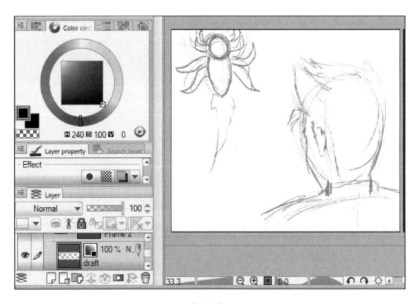

If you want to see exactly what Manga Studio did when we clicked on the Play icon, click on the triangle icon next to the **Create draft layer** option in the **Auto action** palette. This will show us the steps that the action went through to create this draft layer.

This particular action is simple. It created a new raster layer named **draft**, changed the use of color in the layer to blue, and then set the layer type to draft. So if we wanted to, we could draw on the draft layer all day, then save to a .jpg file, but we would get a white image because the draft layer doesn't export. It's only there for our reference, and is a great way to make initial rough sketches. Even if you forget to turn the layer off after your ink and color is over it, or under it, it won't matter because it doesn't show on your final image.

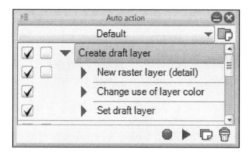

This is just one of the simpler examples of an Auto action. Some of them cover far more extensive sets of steps. Either open an image or select part of the image that you're working on with the marquee tool if you don't currently have a blank canvas open. Then select the **Cut selected area and paste in another layer** action and click on the Play icon.

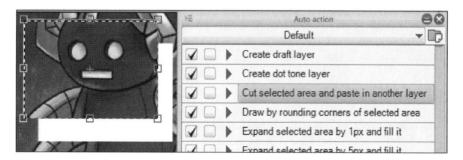

If you want to see how complex an action can get, let's take a look at the **Bevel and Emboss** option. For complex shapes this action isn't always perfect, but it's a lot easier than trying to get this effect by completing the steps yourself or having to put the image in another graphics editing software package.

Make a new layer and drag out a selection with one of the marquee tools. Then navigate to **Edit | Fill** and fill the selection in with a color. Deselect your shape. Then run the **Bevel and emboss** action. Once you've done that, click on the arrow next to the action to see the steps that Manga Studio went through. As you can see, it's quite a list of things that you would have to do manually without the Auto action!

Bevel and emboss makes layer copies, changes blending modes, moves layers, and combines all that mess back to one layer! Phew! It would be a pain to do all of that manually, huh?

You can see in the following screenshot, the list of steps that the Bevel and emboss action go through to create the effect:

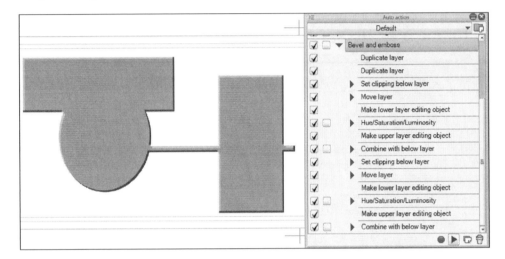

If you're a real stickler for perfectly beveled corners on a complex image like the one in the example, use the eyedropper tool and polygon lasso tool to fix the edges. It will take a little more time, but not as much as you would have spent getting the whole rest of the effect by hand. Simply set the editing layer to preserve transparency, then select the colors of the edges of your beveled shape and correct them by hand. Refer to the following screenshot:

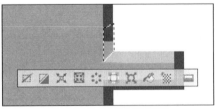

So now that we've seen a few Actions in, well, action, how about we make some of our own?

Creating custom actions

In order to understand how to create our own actions, we must talk about three things: An **Action Set** is a category of actions. An **action** is a series of steps. A **Step** is a process within an action, such as creating a layer, expanding a selection, or adjusting a combine mode or color value. We'll talk about Action Sets first, then we'll talk about making an action and recording steps in the next section.

Action sets

Remember back in *Chapter 3*, *Palettes of a Different Color*, when we discussed making custom color sets? Action sets are pretty much the same thing—a folder storing different actions. You could make an action set for each project that you're working on, or just make one set named Custom where you store the ones that are unique to the way that you work. Or maybe you want to divide them out into Print and Web actions, with different steps for resizing images for display on the Internet or for publication.

For the time being, let's make a set just to store the custom sets of actions that we'll make in the following lessons. In the **Auto action** palette, click on the **Create new auto action set** icon to the right of the **Default** set name. A window will come up for you to input a name for your new set. Let's name it Custom Actions, then hit **OK**, as shown in the following screenshot:

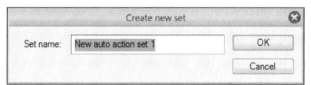

Now in our **Auto action** palette we have two Action Sets, one for the **Default** actions and another for the ones that we'll be making on our own as shown in the following screenshot:

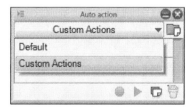

Your **Custom Actions** set is empty right now, but we're going to change that by recording steps to make some Auto actions for our projects. Ready?

Recording an auto action

We're going to start with something simple for our first Auto action. Most comic work is inked, so we're going to have Manga Studio set up an inking layer for us and convert our sketch layer into a draft layer automatically. Setting up a layer to ink on is something that most of us do with every comic page that we create, so it makes sense to have the program do the work for us, right? Even if it saves only 30 seconds, it's still 30 seconds that you don't have to spend fiddling with menus and you can concentrate on your work. Over weeks and months, that time adds up too!

First we'll have to make a new action. Click on the menu at the top left of the **Auto action** palette and select the **Add auto action** option. A new action will be made in the set. **Name your action** and hit *Enter*.

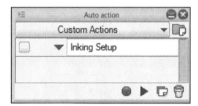

Before we record our action, make sure that you have an image open! We'll be manipulating some layers and we can't do that without layers to do it on, right? I'm working on a sketch that I did previously that could use some inking, and I have my top sketch layer selected.

Once you're ready to start recording your action, hit the Record icon at the bottom of the **Auto action** palette. Now anything that you do to your image is going to be recorded so it can be played back.

Think through your steps before recording an action, to make sure that you have a plan for the most efficient way to get to whatever result you want.

We're going to set our sketch layer to a draft layer first. Either right-click on your layer and go to **Layer Settings | Set as draft layer**, or go to the **Layer** menu at the top of Manga Studio and go to **Layer Settings | Set as draft layer**. To the right of the layer name in the **Layers** palette, a blue pencil icon will appear to show that this is now a draft layer. Then, in the **Layer property** menu, click on the blue square to change the lines on the sketch layer to a blue color. Refer to the following screenshot:

You can see in the **Auto action** palette that the two steps we've done so far are listed under the **Inking Setup** action, which we're developing. This shows us that the steps are being saved, so we can continue.

To finish up, make a new **Raster layer** and rename it. Once you're done, hit the Stop Recording icon at the bottom of the **Auto actions** palette. Your action should have the following steps listed under it:

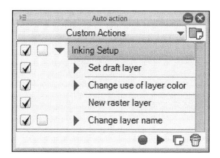

Now, let's open up a different sketch and see if your action is working properly. Open another image and click on the Play button at the bottom of the **Auto action** palette. The steps that we went through on our previous image will happen on our current image, without us having to do any of the work!

If you wish to be able to input the layer name each time the action runs, open the action so that you can see the individual steps. Then click on the checkbox next to the **Change layer name** step. Any time that this step is run, you will see the options for the layer before the action continues playing. Refer to the following screenshot:

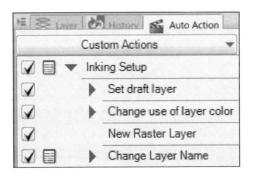

So now we know how to set up a simple action. What else can we make auto actions do? How about setting up a file to make some cel-style coloring insanely easy?

Easy cel-shading coloring with auto actions

To make this action, you'll need an image that you want to color, of course! Filling in the base colors on your image will make it easier to see what this setup is doing because it involves making two tonal adjustment layers and then drawing on the layer masks to reveal and hide parts of the tone correction for the shading. You can put all the base colors on one layer together.

Make sure to fill in areas that are white if using this coloring method. I like a very light gray for the base color on white areas so that white highlights will show up on it.

I'll be using this cute cartoon corgi dog that I drew to show you this action. Looking in the **Layers** palette, you can see that I have an Ink layer, and one layer with all my base colors on it. The white marks on the dog are a very light gray (Hue 0, Saturation 0, Value 96).

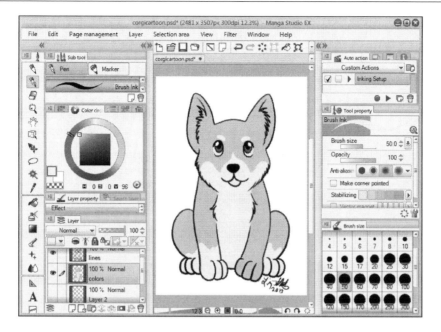

The first thing we need to do is add our new Action. Click on the menu on the top left of the **Auto action** palette and select **Add new action**. Let's name this one Cel Shading. Once you have the name selected, go ahead and hit the Record icon.

First we're going to make our tonal correction layer for our shadows. Go to **Layer | New Correction Layer | Hue/Saturation/Luminosity**. The image that you're working on may require different numbers than the one used for this Corgi art. I settled on -6 on **Saturation** and -10 on **Luminosity** as shown in the following screenshot. Double-click on the adjustment layer in the **Layers** palette and rename it to Shadows.

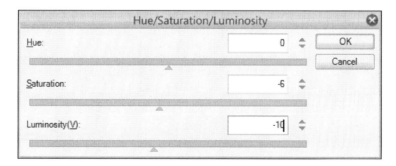

Now, since we've used an adjustment layer, it's also affecting the white background. Right now though we're going to set up the Layer Mask, that is, with the adjustment layer so that all the darker colors are hidden. We'll do more with them later.

Make sure that the **Layer Mask** option on your adjustment layer is selected. The Layer Mask is the rectangle to the right of your layer preview, which for the adjustment layer is simply gray. Layer Masks hide or reveal what's on the layer depending on the color pixel that is drawn on the mask. White shows the layer and black hides it. Layer Masks are incredibly useful to erase something that you don't want to actually delete. No pixels are actually removed from the canvas, they're just hidden.

Say that you had a picture and you cut a window in a piece of black construction paper. When you laid the black paper over the picture, all you would be able to see through is the white space or the holes in the mask. So think of your Layer Mask as a digital piece of paper that you can cut holes in or replace bits of, to hide or reveal what's on the layer.

Click on the **Layer Mask** option to ensure that it is selected. Then use *Ctrl + A* or **Selection Area | Select All** to select your entire canvas. Press *Delete*. The layer mask will become black in the layers palette, indicating that the contents of the layer have been hidden.

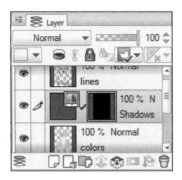

The preview of our Layer Mask is now completely black, and none of the darker colors are showing. This is exactly what we want, so now we can move on to the next step.

Using the same process as before, we are now going to make another **Hue/ Saturation/Luminosity** adjustment layer. This time though, increase the **Luminosity** instead of decreasing it. My Corgi dog required about a +30 Luminosity before I was happy with the colors. Rename this layer to `Highlights`. Then make sure that the Layer Mask is selected. Use **Select All** on the mask and press *Delete*.

Your **Layer** palette should look like the one in the following screenshot:

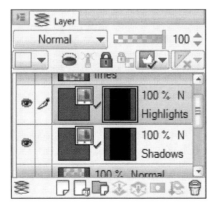

Now hit Stop recording on our **Auto action** palette as that was the last step we needed to complete for our custom action. In order to do your coloring, take a pen or a brush tool and select one of your layer masks. Then simply draw on it with the pen or brush to reveal parts of the hidden pixels, which will bring back the darker and lighter colors depending on the layer mask you draw on. I used the same inking brush that we made back in *Chapter 2, The Right Tools for the Job*, to make little highlights and shading on the dog's ear. Refer to the following screenshot:

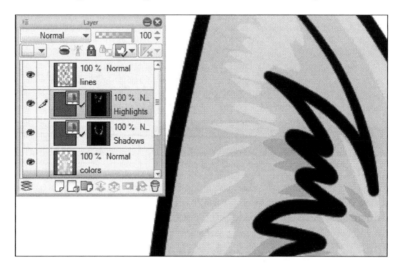

You don't have to use this technique just for cel-style shading, by the way. You can grab one of the soft brush tools and use it to create a more subtle, blended look too. In the following screenshot, the left half of the Corgi was shaded using the inking brush, and the right side was shaded using an oil brush on the layer masks. It gives a much more painted look than using the pen tool and is very subtle.

Now we can open any other file that has base colors set down and run this action to set up our shading and highlighting colors just by selecting our action and hitting Play. The following screenshot was prepared with the same exact settings that were used when we set up the Cel Shading action.

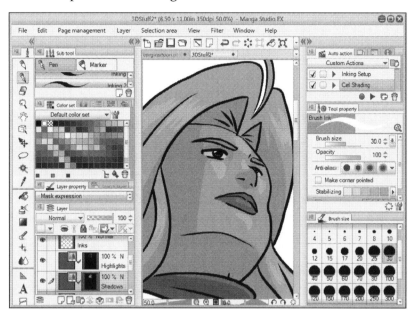

Making line art from a photo

The next action that we're going to learn how to make, is one that will take a photo and give you this effect from it. The photo is shown in the following screenshot:

This mimics a filter that was in Manga Studio 4 called **2DLT**, that created linework from a photograph. You can get the same effect in Manga Studio 5, and with actions you can set it up once and then apply it to any photograph that you wish.

Start off with a single-layered image, such as a photograph from your digital camera. **Add a new auto action** to your **Auto action** palette, and name it `Line Drawing`. Go ahead and hit the Record icon.

Our first step is to duplicate our image layer. Right-click on the image in the **Layers** palette and select **Duplicate Layer**. Or go to **Layer | Duplicate Layer** at the top of your program window.

Your new layer will be on top of the original one. With this layer selected, change the blending mode from **Normal** to **Glow Dodge**.

Next up, go to **Edit | Tonal Correction | Invert Gradation**. You're going to end up with a photo that looks like the following screenshot, which doesn't look like it could possibly ever get to the effect that we're going for, but trust me, it does! Refer to the preceding screenshot.

There is a **Tonal Correction** layer for Invert Gradation, but while testing the steps for this action I found that it didn't give the same effect as using the **Edit-Tonal Correction** menu. In fact, if a **Correction** Layer was used for this effect, I wouldn't get the line-drawing look at all!

Next we need to run the **Gaussian Blur** filter. This will start to give us the line effect, but with colors. A 15-20 setting on the blur seems to be about right, usually. You may have to change this depending on the resolution of the image. Refer to the preceding screenshot.

Once you have the **Gaussian Blur** run, you'll have this:

Pretty close to the line drawing look that we want, right? Now we just need to get rid of the pesky color. (Though if this is the effect that you're going for, by all means, stop right here and leave it just like this. Looks cool, doesn't it?)

In order to take away the color and leave us with a line drawing look, we're going to navigate to **Layer | Tonal Correction Layer | Binarization**. Pull the slider to the left or right until you're happy with the look, and then hit **OK** as shown in the following screenshot:

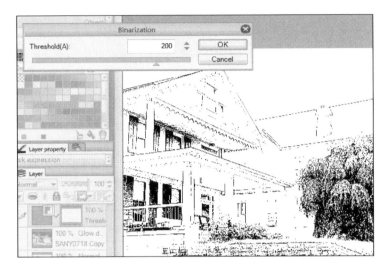

Now you can hit the **Stop Record** button on your **Auto action** palette to cease recording your steps. I have found that the Binarization step needs to be adjusted for most individual images. If it isn't already, open the action that you just made so that you can see the steps. This is done by clicking on the Play icon next to the action name in the **Auto action** palette. Next to the **Binarization** step is a check-box. Click on it and an icon that looks like a notepad will replace the empty box. Whenever this action is run from now on, you will be prompted to set the Binarization levels with the same slider as before.

Now you can run this action on photos galore! In the following screenshot, the panel backgrounds have all been made from photographs and then inserted into the comic.

A few last thoughts on actions

There are three other small things that we should cover about actions, and then we can get on to the fun part of the book: combining everything that we've learned into one big, crazy project! So stick with me for another few minutes on this subject and then we'll get down to more of drawing and creating.

Playing part of an action

There are two ways to play only parts of an action. The first way is to open the action so that the steps are visible and then check or uncheck the boxes to the left of the step names to turn them on or off. Say that we only wanted to make the **Shadows** layer in our cel-shading action. We could open the action and uncheck each step beyond when the layer name for the shadow layer is changed. Then only the steps that are checked will be played as shown in the following screenshot:

If we wanted to play only the steps from the middle of the action onward, we could leave everything turned to on (checked), but select the second **Hue, saturation, and luminosity layer** and hit play. Everything from the selected step on to the end of the action will then be applied to the image.

Setting keyboard shortcuts

For the action that you use over and over again, it makes a lot of sense to pair it to a keyboard shortcut so that you can run it with the press of one button rather than having to go to the **Auto action** palette each time you want to use it. One of the most useful actions that comes built into Manga Studio is the **Expand selected area by 1 px and fill it** action. (And, by extension, the **Expand selected area by 5 px and fill it** one too, since they both do the same thing with a different amount of expansion to them).

Setting actions to a key is easy. Under **File**, go to **Shortcut Settings**. The dropdown menu at the top of the window pulls up different areas of Manga Studio that you can edit the shortcut settings for, such as the tools, file operations, and main menu. If **Auto action** is not already selected in the dropdown, select it. You will see two folders, one marked **Default** and one with **Custom Actions**, which has all the actions that we've used in this chapter. Let's set the two **Expand** and **Fill** actions to the keys *F6* and *F7*.

Expand the **Default** set by clicking on the triangle to the left of the set name. Highlight the **Expand selected area by 1 px and fill it** action, then click on the **Edit Shortcut** button. A blank white box will appear next to the action name. Press the *F6* key on your keyboard. Then click on the **Expand selected area by 5 px and fill it** action name, select **Edit Shortcut**, and press the *F7* key.

When you are done setting your shortcuts, click on **OK**.

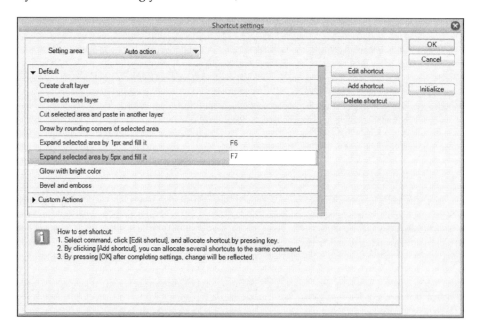

If you want to have multiple keyboard shortcuts for the same action, tool, and so on, simply use the **Add Shortcut** button instead as shown in the preceding screenshot. This will allow you to set up several keys all to activate the same operation.

If you select a shortcut already in use by Manga Studio, it will warn you and ask if you want to overwrite the previous setting as shown in the following screenshot:

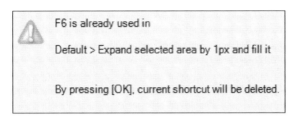

Importing and exporting action sets

Full action sets can be imported and exported through the **Auto action** palette. Simply click on the menu in the top left corner and select **Export Action Set**. A **Save** dialog box will appear. Choose where you wish to save your action set and rename it if you wish.

Then you can take your actions to another computer with Manga Studio, and click on **Import Action Set** from the menu. Navigate to your saved file and click on **Open**. Your actions will be imported for you, so no need to remake your actions if you have several workstations!

Summary

I hope that now you have some ideas for actions that you can record to make your life easier and to streamline your workflow. In this chapter we learned how to:

- Use actions
- Record custom actions
- Playback only parts of actions
- Import and export action sets
- Set actions to shortcut keys

Now we're ready to take everything that we've covered in the past seven chapters and throw it all together to make some comics. So let's do it!

8

Rulers and Speech Balloons

If you're creating comics, you're going to need to use speech balloons. And if you're creating art digitally, you're going to sometimes need the function of a ruler inside your drawing program. Thankfully, that's what this chapter is all about!

This chapter will focus on:

- Working with pre-set word balloons
- Creating custom word balloons
- Using the word balloon pen
- Perspective rulers
- Concentric circle rulers
- Other special rulers
- Guides

We have a lot of ground to cover, so let's get started!

Rulers

A ruler is a great thing to have. And in digital art it's really great, especially if you have a traditional tablet where you aren't looking at the screen in order to draw. Manga Studio comes with lots of ruler options, one of which we've already explored back in the section about word balloons.

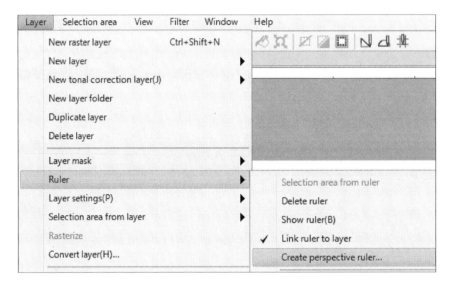

The second page of the little script that we're working on here has a few shots that require drawing backgrounds. For this purpose, using a perspective ruler will make our job infinitely easier.

For the first panel of page two, where Steven Strange is coming into the police station, we'll add a one point perspective ruler to assist us in getting the lines just right. Go to **Layer | Ruler | Create perspective ruler**. Then, in the dialog box that comes up, select the **1 point perspective** and click on the **OK** button. Leave the **Create new layer** checkbox selected and the ruler will be created on its own layer instead of on our sketch layer. Refer to the following screenshot:

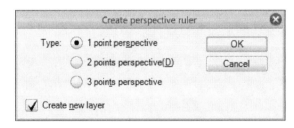

Alright, now we have three lines on our canvas that Manga Studio generated. One is the horizon line, and the other two are the lines for our vanishing point. These are guidelines that will help us get our ruler lined up in exactly the right spot.

Using the Manga Studio perspective rulers is easiest if you know how to draw in a perspective with pencil and paper. If you aren't familiar with how to draw in perspective already, look up tutorials online or get a book or two on the subject. Good backgrounds start with solid perspective, and good backgrounds make for a great comic!

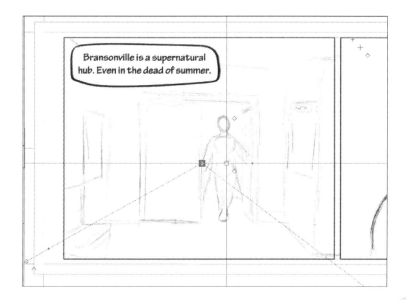

We're going to move the horizon line and the vanishing point lines into place now. Refer to the preceding screenshot. This is much easier if you already have a sketch prepared. Use the **Object selection** tool and click on the blue dot where all the lines meet. Drag this into position where your vanishing point should be.

On the vanishing lines there is a circle. Click on that and drag it in order to reposition the line. The following screenshot shows this. Also, I decided that I wanted the vanishing point in the exact center of the frame. After finding the center, the vanishing point was moved.

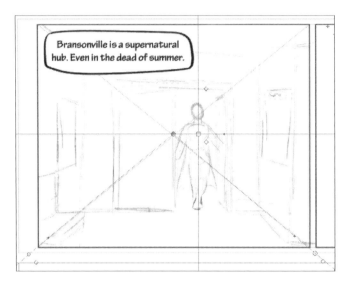

With the ruler in place, and with the ruler layer visible, any lines that we draw will snap automatically to the perspective lines, as well as the horizontal and vertical. This makes doing accurate perspective a cinch because all of your lines are guaranteed to be on the correct diagonal. Refer to the following screenshot:

On this same page, for the background behind Martha, consisting of the front desk attendant in the third frame, we can use another perspective ruler to do the background. This time though we need a **2 point perspective** ruler instead of a one point. To add a two point ruler, perform the same procedure as we did to add a **1 point perspective** ruler, as explained in the beginning of the chapter, but on the dialog box for the ruler we'll select **2 point perspective** and click on **OK**. This time though we will have a horizontal line and two vanishing points as shown in the following screenshot:

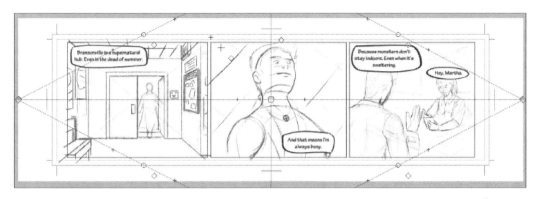

Obviously these vanishing points are nowhere near the place where we need them to be to follow the sketch for the third panel. Use the **Object** selector under the **Operation** tools to move around the horizon line and the vanishing points. The blue square in the center moves the horizon line, the blue circles on either side are the vanishing points. The easiest way, I have found, to get a perspective ruler lined up is to start on one side and get one set of diagonals, where they need to be. Then concentrate on the second vanishing point (and, if you're using a **3 point perspective** ruler, the third point as well!).

Selecting the blue circle allows you to move the vanishing point along the horizon line. The white circles down the diagonal lines are controls for them. Think of the purple diagonals as being guidelines so that you can tell if your vanishing points are in the right spots.

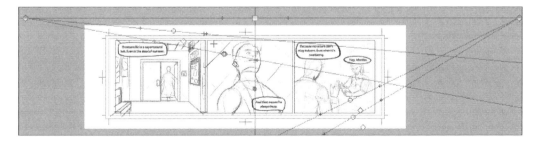

Here's what the whole ruler looks like when set up. Let's zoom in so that you can see exactly where the vanishing points are lined up with the sketch. Refer to the following screenshot:

The right hand vanishing point used the letter tray on Martha's desk to get it lined up. Then the left hand vanishing point was adjusted to the back wall and desks. This is why it's so important to understand drawing perspective first, and then doing a rough sketch before putting down rulers. I find it very difficult to put down rulers and get them in the right positions without guidelines first.

Now we can use our **2 point perspective** ruler to finish our background as shown in the following screenshot:

Once you have the layout of the background done, turn the perspective ruler off and add some details that aren't directly on the vanishing lines. Especially for indoor, habituated spaces, this will make them seem more alive and lived in.

I've sketched in some details on Martha's desk, and added some objects, chairs, and people to the room in the back. This adds more visual interest to the scene and makes it seem less like an empty room that's been drawn with a ruler. People, unless they're extreme neat freaks, don't set things down in perfectly straight lines. So putting pencils, cell phones, notes, and other knick-knacks askew will add to the realism. The room that we prepared can be seen in the following screenshot:

Other functions of perspective rulers

You may notice that the horizon line of our ruler is... well... horizontal. And sometimes when you're doing comics you have an interesting camera angle. If you read mainstream comics you've seen some of these tilted horizon lines, in superhero stories especially. Manga Studio will allow you to tilt the horizon line, you just have to know how to do it.

Let's make a new canvas and add a two point perspective ruler to it. Click on the light blue square at the center of the ruler and drag with your mouse or stylus. The center point will go up and down, and left to right, but will only stay straight. Click on one of the light blue circles and drag it around as well. Try to drag the left-hand circle up while the right-hand one stays put, so that the horizon line will tilt. Manga Studio will probably move the horizon line instead, unless we tell it to not do that.

Right-click on the ruler and a new menu will appear as shown in the following screenshot:

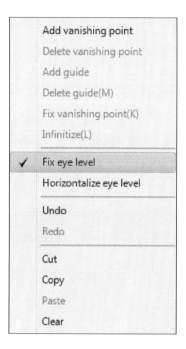

This has all sorts of handy things for our ruler. Right now though, deselect the **Fix eye level** option by clicking on it. Now select the right handle, making sure that the light blue circle is highlighted by a red square. Then drag the handle up and the horizontal line will tilt to the left. Refer to the following screenshot:

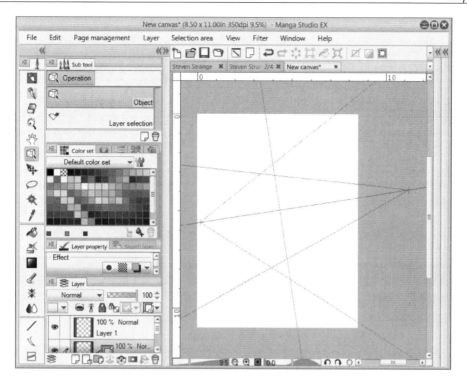

Now we have a much more dynamic angle and can draw our buildings as shown in the following screenshot:

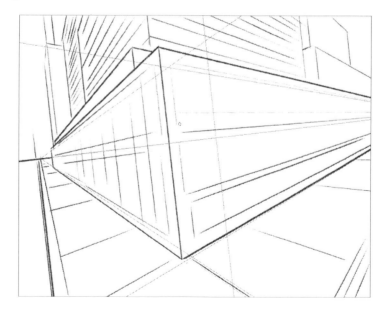

If you change your mind about the eye level and want to go back to it being perfectly horizontal again, simply right-click on your ruler and select the **Horizontalize eye level** option. This resets the horizon line and makes it easier to start again on your ruler if you need to.

What if you're working on a scene and suddenly realize that you need a three point ruler instead of a two point? Rather than recreating the whole ruler from scratch, you can right-click on your current ruler and select **Add vanishing point**. Now we can have a third vanishing point to draw off of, like I've done, as shown in the following screenshot:

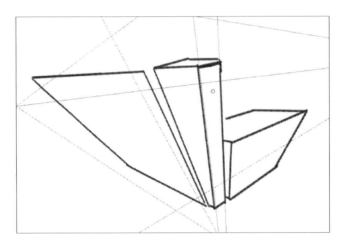

There is nothing more frustrating than getting a vanishing point exactly where you want it, and then accidentally moving it when trying to move something else. To stop that from happening, you can right-click on a vanishing point and the select the **Fix vanishing point** option. This will lock the selected point, and the only way to reposition it is to right-click on it again and deselect the **Fix vanishing point** option.

By default, each vanishing point has two guides that you can use to line up your positions. But if you want more guides, you can add them. To add a guide, click on the white circle control for one of the existing guides. Then right-click and click on **Add guide**. The new guide will be created almost right on top of the existing one, but you can then reposition the guide to where you need it.

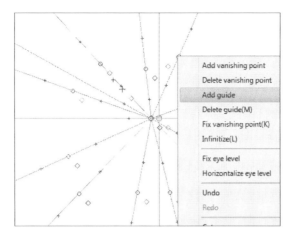

As you can see in the menu, you can also **Delete guides, Delete vanishing points** that you don't want any more, or **Fix the horizon line** so that it can't be moved from where you've put it as shown in the preceding screenshot.

Need to move a ruler from one canvas to another? No problem. Right-click on the ruler and select either **Cut** or **Copy**. Then go to the canvas you wish to transfer the ruler to and right-click on it again. Select the **Paste** option and your ruler will be inserted into the canvas. Refer to the following screenshot:

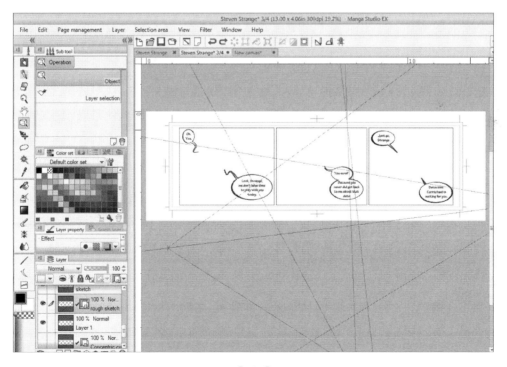

The other rulers

So we've talked a lot about perspective rulers because they're the most complicated ones in Manga Studio. But there are lots of other rulers that you can add to your project to assist you with your drawing. So let's go over those real fast and you'll be familiar with the options for them.

Under the **Figure** (U) tool, go to the **Ruler** sub tool. Select the **Linear** sub tool, then left-click and drag the mouse in your canvas area. You could probably figure it out from the name of the tool, but this ruler produces straight lines. Draw out some straight lines, then take a drawing tool and draw on your canvas. The drawing tool will follow the ruler lines that you laid down.

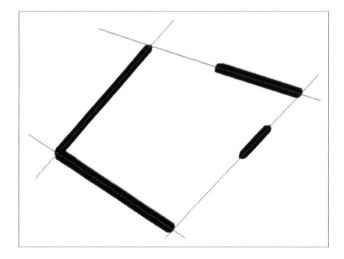

The **curve** ruler will make, of course, curves. Sort of like having a set of French curves that are infinitely customizable. Select the **Curve** ruler from the **Ruler** sub tool menu. Click on where you want to start your curve. As you move your cursor, a line will come out from the first point that you click. Click on the second point of your curve and then keep moving your mouse. The ruler will continue to grow, and as you drag out and move toward a third point the line will curve. Getting used to drawing curves with the curve ruler takes some doing, but with some practice you'll become a pro at it. Continue dragging out lines and clicking points. When you want to end your ruler, either double-click on your final point or connect back to the first place where you clicked.

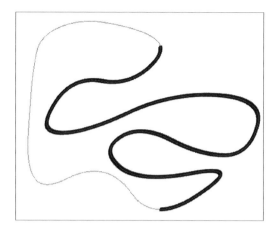

Lines and custom curves are great, but what about squares, circles, and polygons, right? For those we want the **Figure** ruler. When you select the **Figure** ruler, check out the **Tool property** palette for some options for it.

This ruler will draw out a square, a circle, or a polygon, depending on the option that you have selected next to the **Figure** text.

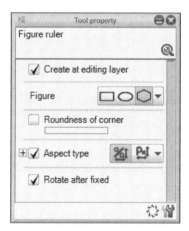

Select a shape and then click on and drag your canvas to create your ruler. Once you've given that a try, click on the **Show [Sub tool detail] palette** icon at the bottom-right corner of the **Tool Property** palette. Click on the **Figure** menu on the left and take a look at the options here.

By default, the **Polygon** ruler will draw a hexagon. However, you will note that in the **Sub tool detail** menu there is an option to change the number of vertices, and therefore the number of sides, on the polygon. If you want access to this option in the **Tool property** palette, rather than having to open the **Sub tool detail** menu any time that you want to change from a hexagon to a triangle, then click on the gray box to the left of the option. When the eye icon appears, that option will show up in the **Tool property** menu for this tool.

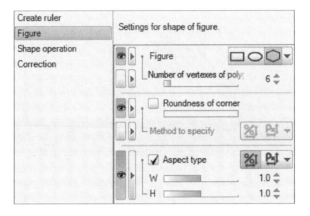

Okay, so let's change the number of vertices to 3 and then drag out a ruler. You will, of course, end up with a triangle! And adding more vertices makes the polygon more complex and have more sides.

Check the checkbox next to **Roundness of corner** and drag out another triangle ruler next to the first one that you made. The default is about 10.0 for the roundness. As you can see, the corners are now soft and rounded. The higher you make the number, the more round the corners will get. The rulers below have been drawn with no corner roundness, 10.0 roundness, 30.0 roundness, and 100.0 roundness. Note that at 100.0 roundness the shape is almost barely recognizable as a triangle because of how soft it has become.

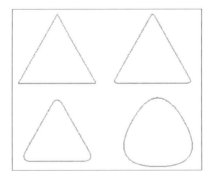

The **Aspect type** control will change the proportions of the ruler that is drawn. By default it's set to a specified ratio of 1:1, which means that parallelogram rulers will always be squares, elliptical rulers will always be circles, and polygon rulers will always have equal sides no matter how large or small you drag them out or how you move the cursor to attempt to skew them. You can set this to different ratios, however, and get rectangular, oval, or other skewed shapes.

The **size** aspect constricts a ruler to a certain size, no matter how far you drag the mouse out. This is a great option if you need a bunch of rulers all the same size—say for windows or inking something mechanical that's repetitive, like rivets or a pattern.

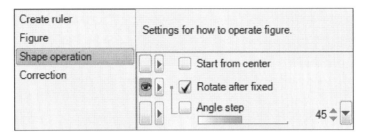

There are a few things under **Shape operation** that we should be aware of, too. The first option under this menu allows you to draw the shape starting from the center, so the center of the ruler will be where you initially click to start dragging out the ruler. **Rotate after fixed** is checked by default, and that means that after you click, drag, and click to set the size of the ruler it will give you the option to rotate it during creation. And the **Angle step** allows you to set a specific angle increment to constrain the rotation to. So say you want to create a bunch of triangle rulers that are all rotated to 30 degrees, you could set that in this option and then draw your rulers out quickly, without having to eyeball the angles.

The ruler pen allows you to create freehand rulers. Simply select this ruler and draw out whatever you wish. Then use it as you would a normal ruler.

There are five different options under the **Special ruler** tool. One of these, the **Concentric Circle** ruler, we've already discussed some when we talked about word balloons earlier in this chapter. But also under this option we have some other useful tools that you can get a lot of use of in your drawings.

First up, there's the **Parallel lines** ruler. Select this option from the drop-down menu in the **Tool property** palette while **Special ruler** is selected. Then click on your canvas and drag the mouse in any direction to draw a line. When you click again, a ruler that has three lines along the line you specified will be drawn.

This is your ruler, however you can draw anywhere on your active canvas while this ruler is active and your drawing tool will follow those lines, making each stroke parallel. Use the **Object** selector to edit the ruler and move or rotate it if you need to take it elsewhere or if your initial mouse clicks weren't accurate.

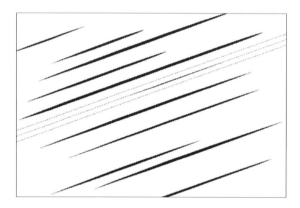

The **Eradiation Line** rulers are a great big time saver if you use Manga style "focus lines" often in your work. Choose this option and then click and drag on your canvas. The ruler that is drawn is a small set of purple lines all radiating from the same central point. You can then use this ruler to draw lines focusing in toward that same point, anywhere on your canvas.

The **Eradiation curve** ruler is the same concept as the **Eradiation line** ruler, except this time it's along a curve that you set. This is good for making quick motion lines or "swirly effects" for special scenes. To make the ruler, select it, left-click on the canvas and drag out a line. Click again to set a point and curve the line. When you double-click the curve will stop and the rest of the ruler will be generated.

Last under this ruler tool are **guides**. Like guides in most graphics software, these are horizontal or vertical lines that you can set up as reference points. However, you can also use drawing tools along them too. So, if you need a perfectly straight across or up-and-down line in a hurry, use a guide instead of the linear ruler. It will just be faster.

Using concentric ruler tools to make word balloons

Under the **Figure** tool menu, select the **Ruler** sub tool. You'll see a list of ruler options, the one that we want is under **Special ruler.** Select it, then under the **Tool property** palette, select **Concentric circle.**

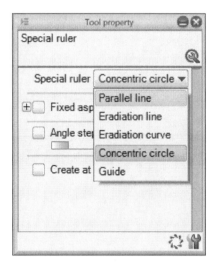

Left-click with the mouse on your canvas and drag while holding the button down. The purple lines that appear are the guidelines of the ruler that you're creating. Don't fuss too much with getting it perfect right off the bat. If it's not quite in the right spot or the right shape, use the **Move Layer** tool or the **Object selection** tool to drag the ruler around to where it needs to be. The **Object selection** will let you tweak the control points of the ruler, too, so you can make it fit your text.

Once you're happy with your ruler, take your custom **Balloon pen** tool and draw around your dialog text.

 If your tool doesn't automatically follow your ruler, make sure that the **Snap to special ruler** option is turned on.

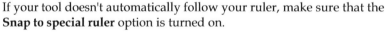
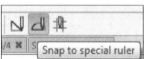

One of the nice things about using a ruler to hand ink your word balloons is that you can put down one **Concentric Circle** ruler and then just spend a little time moving it around to each bit of text that you need to draw a balloon around. Use your balloon pen around the ruler, then move the ruler layer again and resize it if you need a different shape.

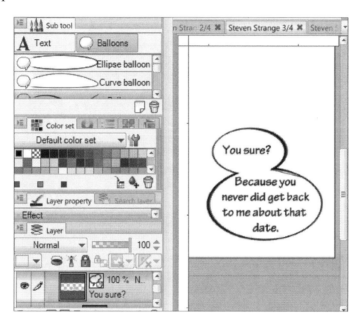

Want to join two balloons together? Layer one over top of the other so that they're overlapping where you want them to join. Then right-click on the top balloon layer and select **Combine with below layer.**

Text and word balloons

So now that I've shown you how to use a concentric circle ruler to make word balloons, what about the other text and word balloon functions of Manga Studio 5?

Depending on how you like to work, text and word balloons might be the first or last thing that you do. For me, it's the first. I like having the text figured out already so that I know how much space there is for art, and if I have to make any edits or shorten lines.

My scripts are usually simple. They can look just like this:

Page One

Panel One: Outside, city.

  Narration: When you're going up against the strange, it helps to be a little strange.

Panel Two: Outside, city.

  Narration: Hi. I'm Steven Strange.

Panel Three: Outside, police station.

  Narration: Welcome to Bransonville. Summer, 2013. During the worst heat wave in recorded history.

Page Two

Panel One: Silhouette against the open police station door.

  Narration: Bransonville is a supernatural hub. Even in the dead of summer.

Panel Two: Close on Steven, wearing a trenchcoat.

  Narration: And that means I'm always busy.

Panel Three: Steven stops at the front desk.

  Narration: Monsters don't stay indoors, even when it's sweltering.

  Steven: Hey, Martha.

Page Three

Panel One: Martha, the front desk woman, looks up from a crossword puzzle. She seems bored.

  Martha: Oh. You. Look, Strange, we don't have time to play with you today.

Panel Two: Steven leaning down, smiling.

  Steven: You sure? Because you never did get back to me about that date.

Panel Three: She hands him a Visitors badge while rolling her eyes.

  Martha: Just go, Strange. Detective Carmichael is waiting for you.

Page Four

Panel One: Inside the station, rows of desks with detectives bustling around.

Panel Two: Steven comes in the room, he is looking left.

Carmichael (off screen): Isn't that coat a little much for this weather?

Panel Three: Steven turning, looking a bit surprised.

Steven: Well hello, Detective.

If you wish to use a script program to do your writing, Celtx is recommended. It's a free software that can be downloaded from `Celtx.com` and it does all sorts of scripts, from screenplays to radio dramas. If you have the writing program Scrivener, it can also be used to do scripts with a template. Use whatever writing software that you'd like though, and add as much detail to your panel descriptions as you need to. Since I'm usually the one drawing my scripts, I don't tend to put too much detail into them unless I have a very specific idea for how I want something to look and want to remember it.

So now that we have our script, we're going to put the narration and dialog in our panels. Once you have the text laid out, it's time for balloons. For this project, we're going to use a freehand look for the narration and an ellipse balloon for the actual dialog.

First, let's handle the narration. You'll find the balloon tools in the same **Sub tool** menu as the text tool. On my Manga Studio, I've actually moved the balloon tools to their own menu, as that makes them easier to sort through when you start to make custom text tools too. Select the **Balloon Pen** tool and draw around the narration text to make your balloon.

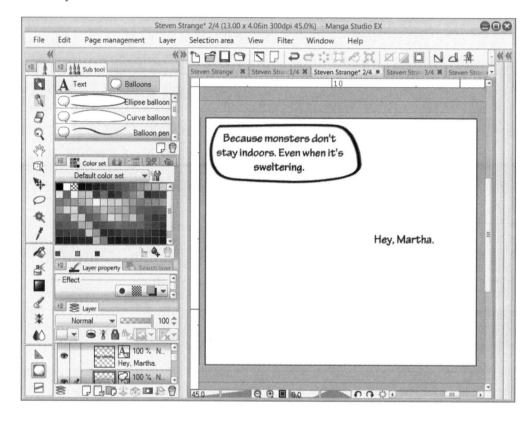

As you can see, we can make custom balloon pens to achieve a rougher look with the pen tool. To do this, select the **Balloon pen** and then click the icon next to the trash can at the bottom of the **Sub tool** menu. This will make a copy of the currently selected tool.

To make the tool above, click on the double wrench icon in the **Tool property** palette. Under the **Brush size** settings, set the input to be determined by **Pen pressure**, and lower the **Minimum value** to about 20. Then under the **Brush tip**, change **Circle** to **Material.** Choose one or two materials for the brush tip that will give you a rough effect.

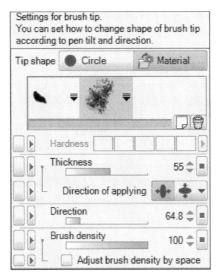

 For more information on making custom tools, see *Chapter 2, The Right Tools for the Right Job.*

Once you have your balloon pen looking the way that you want it, go ahead and draw around your narration text. It doesn't have to be perfect, not with the look that we're going for on the Steven Strange pages anyway. Once we have the narration text outlined and we like our tool, we can use the ellipse balloon on the dialog. Select the ellipse balloon and drag out an oval around your line of dialog.

Perhaps, though, we want the dialog balloon to match the style of the balloon pen a bit more. Right now it is a bit jarring to have the dialog balloon with that steady line width all around it. So let's use the ruler function of Manga Studio, along with the balloon pen tool that we made, to make an ellipse around the dialog instead.

Balloon tails

I have a confession here—balloon tails are usually one of the last things that I do. That way I can make sure they match up with the art that I've drawn. But since we're talking about balloons, let's talk about the tails while we're at it. Manga Studio already comes with two preset options for tails, under **Balloon tools**.

The **Balloon rounded tail** option will produce the classic "thought bubble" tail, like this:

While the **Balloon tail** will produce one of the typical tails used when a character is speaking. The following example is the **Balloon tail** set to the **Linear** option.

Both tail tools also have two other options for how to bend, **Polyline** and **Spline**. To use these, change the **How to bend** mode in the **Tool property** palette using the drop-down menu. Then click inside your word balloon and drag out the first part of your tail. Click where you want your bend to start and pull in another direction. You can continue doing this as many times as you wish. When you are finished, double-click at the end of your tail.

Oh, and you can even freehand your balloon tails if you want. Select the **Balloon** pen again and draw a tail over your balloon. Make sure to close the shape.

Use the **Object selection** tool and double-click on the balloon or the balloon tail to edit the individual points and smooth it out if you need to. This is much faster than trying to draw a perfect tail!

Once you have a shape that you like, right-click on the layer that was created by the **Balloon** pen and select **Combine with below layer**. The tail will automatically be joined with the main part of the balloon.

Summary

As you can tell, Manga Studio has a lot of tools that can make your comic and illustration work a lot more efficient. In this chapter we discussed:

- Working with word balloons
- Creating custom word balloons
- Using the word balloon pen
- Perspective rulers and how to use them
- Concentric circle rulers
- Other special rulers, like the eradiation ruler and curve rulers
- Guides

Now that we've discussed a lot of the tools that can make you a Manga Studio Master, it's time to go on to the next chapter and start putting all our knowledge together!

9
Putting It All Together!
Drawing and Inking

We've almost come to the end of our journey together, and now it's time to put everything we've learned together. The next two chapters are going to recap the techniques we've learned while creating a four page comic strip.

This chapter will focus on:

- Creating a four page file using the Story creator
- Using custom actions to set up layers
- Inserting panels using custom materials
- Posing a 3D model to use for sketching
- Inking with a custom inking pen

We've got a lot to do, so we'd better hop to it!

Creating our file

First of all we'll need to obviously create our file. We're going to use the standard newspaper style comic strip template that we created back in *Chapter 1, Getting Familiar with the Story Features*. Just in case you don't remember, or didn't save the dimensions, here they are again:

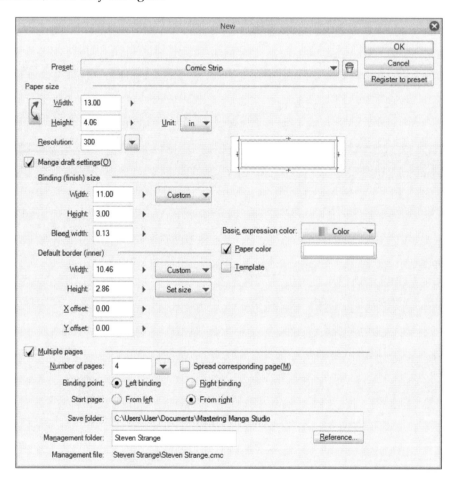

Under the **Multiple pages** option, be sure to select 4 for your **Number of pages**. We don't need to do a two-page spread so that box can be left unchecked. Since I'm an English speaker, I'll be putting the binding on the left and the **Start page** on the right. The **Reference** button allows you to navigate to a folder to store your file. Be sure to also enter a name in the **Management folder** textbox before clicking on **OK**. Manga Studio needs to know where you'd like the page files to be saved, after all!

Double-click on **Page 1** to open the canvas.

Using materials to lay out frames

On the first strip we're going to manually lay out our frames, and then we're going to save the layout as a Material and apply it to our other three pages to save time. In order to use the **Cut frame border** tool, we have to make a **Frame folder** layer. Under the **Layer** menu, go to **New Layer | Frame Folder.** In the **New Frame Folder** dialog box, click on **OK.** The area on the outside of the Default Border that we set up will turn blue. The white area inside is the only panel that is set up now, so we have to use the **Cut frame border** tool to divide the space into three frames.

The **Cut frame border** tool is under the **Correct Line** tool menu (keyboard shortcut: *Y*). Under the **Tool property** you can set the width of the gutter between the panels. Mine is set to 25 for both the horizontal and 24 for the vertical space. Hold down the left mouse button and drag to draw your gutter between the frames. Holding down *Shift* will constrain the panel gutter to become perfectly horizontal or vertical.

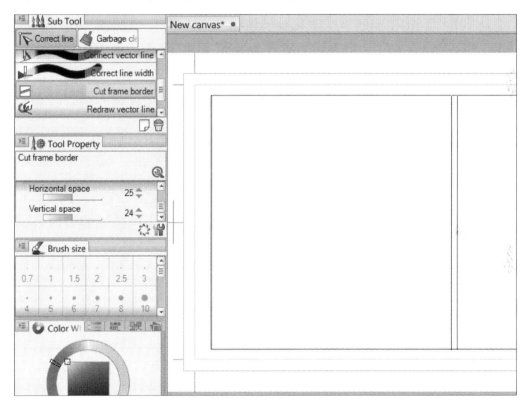

Use the **Cut frame border** tool to divide the white space in to three equal panels. You can use the **Object Select** tool to resize the frames later if they're not even. Refer to the following screenshot:

Once we're happy with the size of our panels, we can save the whole layout as a Material and use it on the rest of our strips. Go to **Edit | Register layer as template material**. Name your new material `Three Panel Strip` and add keywords so that you'll be able to search for it later. We'll store this in the **Manga material | Framing template** folder as shown in the following screenshot:

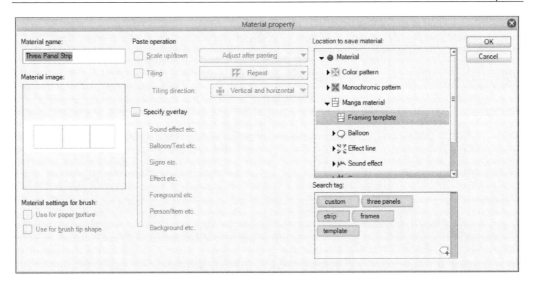

After clicking on **OK** on the **Material property** window, go back to the tab with all four of your pages listed in Manga Studio and double-click on **Page 2**. Open the **Materials** palette and find the layout that we just made. Paste it on to the second page of the file. Refer to the following screenshot:

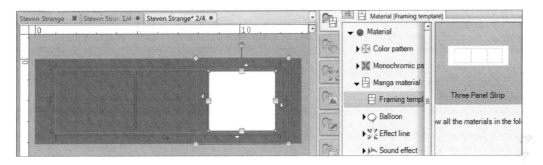

Now you can do the same for the other two strips in the file as well. And just as easy as that, our file is ready for us to start drawing in our panels! Refer to the following screenshot:

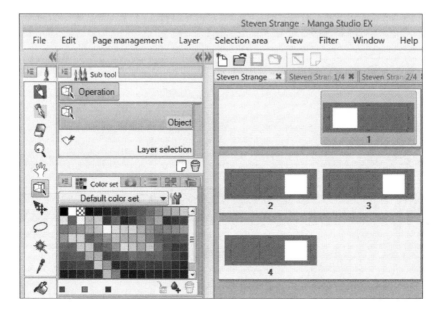

Drawing

Okay, now we have our frames set up and our text finished. Time to move on to drawing! First, we'll need to set up our layers for sketching so that we're ready to go on each page.

Using actions to set up sketching layers

If there's one thing I always end up doing over and over again on my digital art, it's setting up at least two layers for sketching. One I use for a rough sketch and a layout. The other is for a more refined sketch. Since I know how I work and that I'll always have at least these two layers, why not make an action to set them up for me to save some time?

Open the **Auto action** palette, either by clicking on it or going to **Window | Auto action** to pull it up. Click on the menu in the top left of the palette and select **Add auto action**. Name it `Layer Prep` and hit *Enter*.

When you make your pages, each one should have a layer named **Layer 1** Make sure that this layer is highlighted in the **Layer** palette before clicking on the **Record** icon in the **Auto action** palette.

Click on the Record icon and then double-click on **Layer 1** in the **Layers** palette. Change the name to Rough Sketch. Set it to a blue-line layer in the **Layer property** palette so that any drawing you do on it will be blue.

> Far too often when you're doing digital art, you will end up inking or drawing on the wrong layer. That's one of the reasons why the Color effect is such a lifesaver in Manga Studio 5. Set your sketch layers to use it, and you'll never end up inking on the wrong layer again. Unless, of course, you ink your drawings in light blue.

Then add a new **Raster layer**. Double-click on it and rename it to sketch. Then select the rough sketch layer. This way, when we play the action it will automatically select that layer that we want to start sketching on. Now click on the Stop icon on the **Auto action** palette.

Go to the other pages in your file and make sure that **Layer 1** is selected. Then play the action that we've just created. Your sketch layers will be made, and now we're ready to draw!

Using 3D elements for sketching

In **Panel 3** of **Page 3** on the Steven Strange comic that we're working on, Martha the receptionist is handing Steven a Visitor's Badge from across her desk. Let's use a 3D model to make sure that we get this pose and the hand positioning correct.

First, we'll need to make sure that we're on **Page 3** of our story file. Go to the **Story** tab and double-click on **Page 3** if it's not already opened. Zoom in a bit so that the third panel is in focus on your screen. Then let's open the **Materials** palette and take a look in the **3D | Pose** folder to see if there's anything that looks close enough to the pose we want for us to use it.

Or, to speed up the process of finding the right pose, let's select a keyword to narrow down the choices. Martha's sitting down, and underneath the option for us to type a keyword in the right side of the **Materials** palette is a list of tags that Manga Studio uses. Scroll down and click on the **Sit_down** tag to highlight it and the results will be restricted to just the poses that have this tag assigned to them. Refer to the following screenshot:

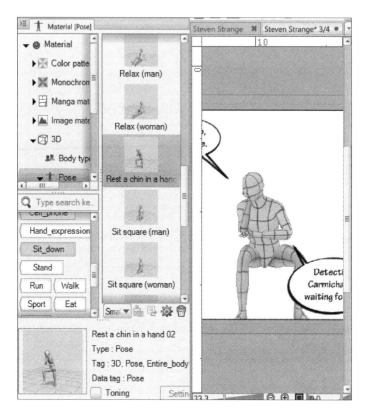

With a little editing, I think that this pose will do just fine. We'll have to turn the head so that she's looking forward at the camera, and we can move the left arm so that it's holding something out towards the viewer. Let's pose the model first and then we'll move the camera.

The easiest part to move is going to be the head. Select it and then use the red control on the circle to angle the face more straightly out so the nose is pointing towards your screen as shown in the following screenshot. We should also use the green control to angle it up, since she's looking at Steven and he's standing while she's sitting down.

If you can't tilt the head up, select the neck joint and move it instead. The head may be up as far as it can go. You may have to zoom in the camera some to get a better view.

That looks good enough for now; we can adjust it later once we get the camera where we want it. Let's work on the arm next. We need to bring the left arm up and rotate the hand around so that the palm is facing up. We'll also need to move the fingers. Select the shoulder joint and rotate it so that the forearm is up and the elbow of the model is resting on the table. Then select the palm and rotate it so that it's facing up instead of down.

As we saw in *Chapter 6, It's Only a (3D) Model*, there's an easier way to move the fingers than rotating each one individually. Under the **Tool property** palette, click on the double wrench icon in the lower-right corner. Then go to the **Pose** menu in the dialog box that appears. If you just rotated your hand then it should be selected already, but if it's not selected, then click on it now so Manga Studio knows which hand you want to control. Refer to the following screenshot:

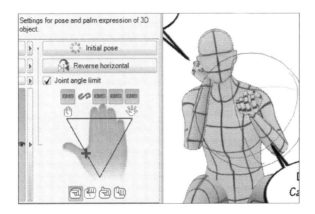

Use the crosshairs in the triangle to pull the fingers, which are most of the way closed as shown in the preceding screenshot. Then lock the pinkie and ring finger by using the chain link icons above them in the control. Open the thumb, forefinger, and middle finger a bit by moving the crosshairs back up towards the top of the triangle.

Keep adjusting the fingers until you have them in a pose that you like. Now we can adjust the camera. Let's zoom in closer so we get a better shot of the character's face. Use the camera controls to zoom in closer and then use the rotation tool in order to get a more interesting angle than just straight on. Refer to the following screenshot:

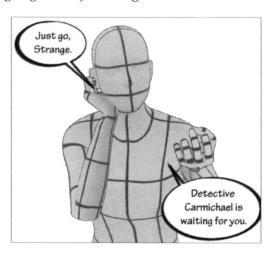

Not sure how to pose the hand? Grab an index card or small piece of paper and imitate the pose to get a feel of it with your own body. Look at your hand and note what you do, then translate it to your character's body position. Sometimes when you draw comics the best way to figure out a pose is to get up and do it yourself. And for facial expressions, study movies and shows, and keep a mirror handy so you can reference your own face.

Now we're ready to go ahead and pencil in the rest of our comic. With the 3D layers, I like to drop the opacity to about 50% or so and draw on a layer over the top of them so I just have the 3D as a reference point. If you have limited RAM on your system, right-click on any 3D layers and rasterize them when you're finished adjusting them to save memory on your computer. Refer to the following screenshot:

Inking

Inking isn't something that you absolutely have to do. If the style or tone of your illustration or comic calls for it, or if your penciling is very tight, you can even skip inking entirely. It's all up to you. Personally, I love to ink. For me, it's one of the most relaxing parts of my process and the part that starts to make it look finished. Perhaps that's because my penciling is usually quite rough and messy, and I fill in a lot of details during the inking process.

To start inking, I set my finished sketch layers to a blue line so that I can see the inks that I'm putting down. Then I create an **inks** layer within the **Frame 1** folder, but below any text layers as shown in the following screenshot:

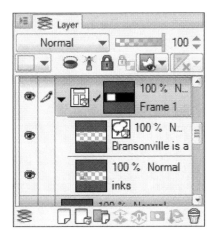

With the **inks** layer here, it will be affected by the Layer Mask on **Frame 1** and so you won't end up with any of your finished lines outside of your panel border.

Now we can take a pen tool and begin to ink the pencil lines. I know that sometimes a lot of artists have trouble with inking, so I'm going to share some tips here that will hopefully help you out if you're one of those that do have issues with inking.

First of all, for backgrounds or mechanical objects, unless the style of your comic calls for it, use a ruler to ink. I save the rulers that I've set up and just turn the layer visibility on and off between drawing and then coming back and inking so it's not in my way. Especially for perspective rulers. This will make it a lot easier when you go back in to ink because all you have to do is turn the layer back on, go to your ink layer, and start inking.

 If your inking tool is not following the ruler, make sure that your **Snap to Special Ruler** option in the top toolbar is selected.

Also, using perspective rulers makes short work of tiled floors, ceilings, or walls. Refer to the following screenshot:

Bransonville is a supernatural hub. Even in the dead of summer.

With the perspective lines all inked, now it's time to turn the ruler off and put in the details.

Something else to keep in mind when inking is: usually you want a thicker line for elements in the foreground and a thinner line for elements in the background. This is not only a principle of learning perspective, but it also helps to draw the reader's attention to the elements that you want them to look at. Reversing this, and putting thinner lines on the foreground objects and thicker on the background can cause visual confusion. Note that the lines on the character in the following image are much thicker than the lines in the background:

The simple drop ceiling tile background in that shot was inked with a parallel line ruler. First, one diagonal was inked, then the ruler layer was selected and the **Object** tool was used to adjust it to the other angle. This results in an interesting, simple, efficient background upon which to introduce our main character. And it only took a minute to draw it!

Let's talk a second about a little principle that will make your ink works more dynamic. It's called **Line Weight**, and it's all about making lines thinner where there's more light (highlights), and thicker where there's less. There are some styles of art that look great with lines that are all the same width (that style of inking is called **Ligne Claire**, by the way), like the art by *Hergé* in *The Adventures of Tin Tin*.

I love inking with line weights. It's just my thing. I think it makes the art pop and can really draw attention to your focal points in your drawings. Line weight applied correctly can also give a sense of light and dark, and the angle from where that light is coming on to the scene. Keep this in mind as you're inking, especially if you're going to color the piece later as you won't want your line weights and your coloring to clash.

When you first start working with line weights, they can be a bit confusing. The main thing to keep in mind is where the light is coming in from in your piece and then ink accordingly. If you need to, put a mark on your sketch layer even to remind you where the light source is and what direction it's going in.

Here's a quick drawing I did of Steven Strange and inked three times. The circle with arrows coming out of it is where the light source is in each version. Note that lines that are further away from the light source are thicker, and have more weight on them than the ones closer to the light.

In the second image, the light source is on the left instead of the right. Note that now the cheek line, top of the nose, and the lapel of the jacket are thinner lines than they were before. The back of the hair though, since the light source is now on the opposite side, is a thick line instead of a thin one.

[On shiny areas, or areas that are very close to a bright light source, break up the thin line to make the effect more dramatic.]

Some areas of the face will almost always be in shadow, unless the lighting is very specific and dramatic. Areas such as under the nose, chin, and brows will usually be in shadow. Unless there is a light source pointing straight up in to these areas, that is.

Note how moving the light source to downward direction, as in the third image, has made the drawing very different. Now the bottom of the chin, the nose, and the brows are inked with a much lighter line. Lighting from underneath is usually very dramatic, so I went with more lines on the face and around the eyes to enhance the look.

The best way to improve your inking though is to practice, and to find an inking tool that you love. Look at the way that comics and art that you like are inked and try to analyze what it is about the style that draws you in. Is it the texture? Is it the weight of the lines and the spot blacks? Pick it apart, really look at it, and then give it a try on your own art.

Summary

I'm so glad that you made it through this chapter. How is your comic looking? I'm sure it's great, and I hope that you're enjoying Manga Studio as much as I enjoy it!

Here are the important points we covered this chapter:

- Setting up a multi-page file using a previously built page template
- Cutting frame borders using the panel cut tool
- Saving the frame borders as a Material and inserting them into the other pages of our file
- Using a 3D model to lay out a character pose
- How to ink, as well as some inking tips and tricks

Now we have a pretty nice-looking comic here. But we can still do more to finish it up, and that's what we're going to talk about in *Chapter 10, Finishing Touches*. Get ready, because toning and coloring is up next!

10
Finishing Touches

In the last chapter we wrote a four page script, set up our file, and then penciled and inked our four pages. Now it's time to address putting the finishing touches on our comic. For some projects, you might be done after the penciling or inking stage. For others, you may need to add tone or color, or both! So in this chapter we're going to learn the following:

- Using screentones
- Setting up layers for coloring
- Setting reference layers for the fill tool
- Making a custom brush to do soft shading
- Blending mode use for the gradient tool

We'll be learning most of that through a comic coloring method that I've been teaching myself for the past few years. I think it's easy enough for anyone to do and get some great results with. So let's finish up our Steven Strange comic!

Screentones

Most traditional black and white Manga are shaded with **screentones**. These tones come printed on sticky clear sheets, and they are applied to sections of the art and then cut in to the shape of the shading. The extra is then peeled away, leaving behind the printed dots. The size and closeness of these shapes, which can be circles, squares, triangles, or anything else really determine how dark the shading looks on the finished product.

The screentone examples in the following screenshot are 5%, 15%, 30%, 50%, 65%, and 90% darkness settings, with the line setting at 60.0 number of lines.

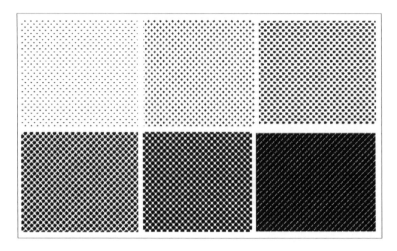

Let's talk about the tone settings first before we get into using them on our comic. There are several ways you can generate screentones in Manga Studio. One way is through the **Materials** palette, and the other is from the bar of icons underneath the marquee when you make a selection.

Create a blank canvas and use the **Rectangle selection** tool to drag out a square. Then in the bar under your selection, click on the New Tone icon. Refer to the following screenshot:

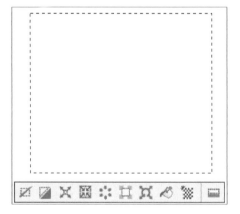

This icon brings up the **Simple Tone** Settings, which we can use to make tones that are not in the preset materials that come with Manga Studio 5.

The **Number of Lines** dropdown changes how many lines of dots there will be within the tone. The larger the number, the more lines there will be, and therefore the smaller the individual dots. Think of this like your DPI settings, the larger the number you have, the more dots per inch you will have. So if you want your tone's individual dots to be more noticeable, leave the number small. If you want them to act more like a solid gray tone, make the number larger.

Density is the percentage of darkness for the tone. A smaller density produces a less intense area of shading because the dots are smaller, and therefore have more white spaces between them. A higher density number has larger dots, so there are less white spaces, and the tone area will be more dramatic and intense.

Type changes the shape of the dots. I keep using the word dots to describe the tones, but they don't have to be just circles. Manga Studio can generate lines, cross-hatching, noise, and even tiny flowers or ninja stars for the screentone. Selecting one of the options from this drop-down menu will show a preview of the pattern:

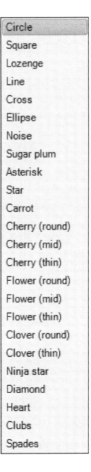

The **Line**, **Cross**, and **Noise** options are the ones that do not produce just a pattern of small dots. **Line** produces just that, straight lines of hatching that will fill the selection. The **Cross** option produces a diamond pattern of lines or cross-hatching. And **Noise** makes a random pattern of black, gray, and white pixels that produces a "cloudy" or "television-static" effect as shown in the following screenshot:

The **Angle** setting controls the angle that the lines of tone will display on. This defaults to 45 degrees, but you can achieve different looks with different angles. Note that in the following screenshots the tone type is **Cherry (Thin)**, and the tone on the left is 45 degrees, while the one on the right is 90 degrees. An angle of 90 degrees gives straight lines horizontally and vertically, of course.

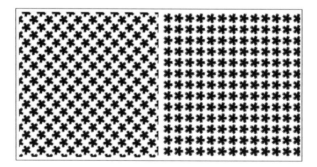

Also at the bottom of the simple tone settings is a checkbox marked as **If there are tones with the same settings, combine them into one(L)**. With this box checked, any tones that are made that have identical settings will be placed on to the same layer. So, you could go back to a character's hair three times and add more tone to areas, but so long as you use the same settings that you did previously the tones will all show up on the same layer. This cuts down on the number of individual layers that you have to sift through, and saves RAM for your computer too.

Let's make a square having a tone of 50.0 number of lines, density of 40%, type circle, and angle setting 45 degrees. Now, what if we wanted to soften the edges of this square so they weren't so straight and well, ridged? Go to the **Pattern Brush** menu and under the **Hatching** sub tool, click on the **Cross-hatching (for tone scraping)** tool. Refer to the following screenshot:

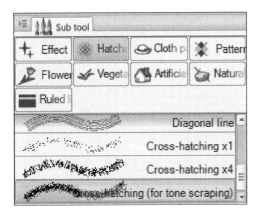

Now take this tool and start using it on your tone's Layer Mask. The pattern of this brush softens and extends the edges of the tone to make them fade out a bit more as shown in the following screenshot:

You can also layer effects and pattern brushes over your tones to get other looks. Here's that same bit of tone, zoomed out so that it's viewed at 25% instead of 50%. Create a new layer over the tone layer and use white and a pattern brush or any two options of your choice to "etch" into the tone as shown in the following screenshot:

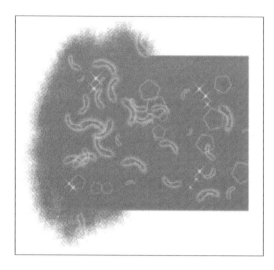

If we don't like that look, we can simply delete the new layer with our feathers and use sparkles on it, and start all over again. **Color** can also be applied under the tone to darken the color or produce other effects. Make or select a layer beneath your tone, and add a **Sunset Glow** gradient. You can see that wherever the tone is present, the color looks much darker than the surrounding color as shown in the following screenshot:

Now that we're familiar with some basic settings for tones, let's open up the **Materials** palette and go to the **Monochromic pattern | Basic** folder. This will show you the basic tone materials that are stored in Manga Studio as shown in the following screenshot:

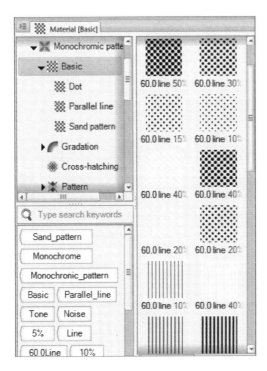

The tone materials default to **60.0** number of lines and come in different densities. There are also tones with white dots instead of black, and a selection of line and noise patterns as well. To use one of these Materials, click on the thumbnail of the Material you wish to use and drag it to the canvas, or click on the **Paste a selected material on the canvas** icon at the bottom of the window that displays the thumbnails. If there is no selection currently active, the selected material will fill the entire canvas.

Let's open up the second page of our Steven Strange comic and fill in Steven's coat with **50%** tone. If we just paste the tone into our page with no active selection, it's going to tone the entire comic and then we would have to erase all the areas in which we don't want to have the 50% shading. That's tedious and a waste of time, so instead we'll make a selection of the coat and just fill that.

There are several ways you could make the selection active. You could use the **Lasso selection** tool and draw around the coat areas. Or you can use the **Auto Select (Magic Wand)** tool. Make sure that you have it set to **Select another layer for reference** and that any sketch layers are turned off. Click in the spaces of the coat of frame 2 to select them. Then expand the selection by a little bit so that the tone will go beneath the inks and not leave a white "halo" around it. Then we can apply the tone and it will just be inside of Steven's coat as shown in the following screenshot:

Of course, we can also make a custom tone using the **Simple tone settings** option that we discussed earlier and save it to the **Materials** palette so that we can use it in other files. Let's make a new canvas; any size will do. Make sure that the **Paper Color** checkbox in the **New Canvas settings** is unchecked though, so that we end up with a canvas that has a transparent background. Select the entire canvas using *Ctrl + A*, or use the rectangle selection tool and drag it over the entire canvas. We don't want to have any unselected space.

Now use the simple tone settings and create a tone that fills the entire canvas. Let's have fun and select the **Stars** type as shown in the following screenshot:

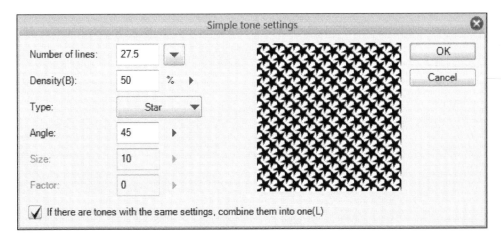

Once we have the settings that we're happy with, click on **OK**. The canvas will be filled with just the black tone and transparent space. Now let's go to **Edit | Register Image as material** to save the tone to our **Materials** palette.

Let's enter the name `27.5 Line 50% Stars` for our **Material name**. I want to specify the overlay (by selecting the **Specify overlay** checkbox) so that this tone always pastes to the background of the canvas, because I'll want it behind any line art layers. Add some tags, and then click on **OK** and your material will be saved. Refer to the following screenshot:

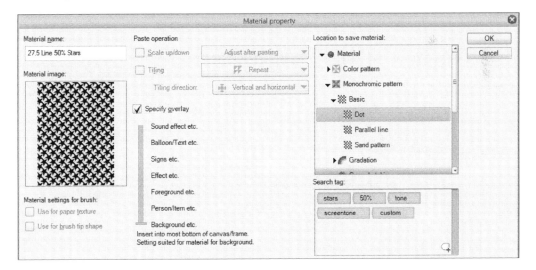

Now the screentone setting will be available from the **Materials** palette whenever you need it. I would recommend doing this for any settings that you're going to be using over and over again, such as a character's clothing or hair style of a character that shows up many times over the course of a comic.

So we know the basics about screentones. Let's work on a few panels with them. How about going back to the second panel of page two and finishing that up. Take the **Lasso selection** tool and select the areas of the face that are going to be shadowed. Refer to the preceding screenshot.

If you ink using line weights, make sure to pay attention to where your thicker lines are to place your shadows. My heavier line weights are on the right side of Steven's face, so the light is coming from the left. With that in mind I've selected the right side of the face, under the nose, and beneath the chin too. Don't forget inside of the ear and under any bits of hair that fall over the forehead or face.

Select the New Tone icon and fill it with about a **40%** density tone. To shade the jacket we can select some shadow areas and fill them with a **75%** density tone because the jacket is filled with 60% already we need to make it darker to look like the shadows on a dark coat. Fill in any other areas that you'd like, such as the shirt and the ceiling tiles.

Zoom out and take a look at your panel to make sure it's how you want it to be. 25% is about a good zoom to preview it, as it prevents the tones from getting a moiré pattern. Refer to the following screenshot:

Looking good so far, but we could push it off further to get some deeper darks out of it and really make the art pop. So let's add some more dark tones to the deep parts of the face and to the contours of the hair. Then we'll add a new raster layer just under the line art, but above the screentones and add highlights to the hair with white. You can also locate the hair screentone layer and use the eraser on it if you'd prefer to keep the number of layers you are working with down to a minimum. Refer to the following screenshot:

Coloring – the comic book style

What I'm about to show you is my absolute favorite coloring method. And I'm going to confess, I hated coloring until I did a lot of experimenting, studying other people's methods, and trial and error to get this method down. Now I love my coloring, and I think that this technique is easy enough that anyone can do it so long as they have a basic understanding of the way that light and shadow fall. Here's an example of the results that you can get with this technique.

Maybe this style of coloring isn't your cup of tea. That's great, don't color in such a manner if you don't like it and if it doesn't fit your art. But reading about this technique might give you some insights or tips that could help you with your own work, so I'd urge you to continue reading.

The first thing that we're going to do for this coloring method is to set up some layers. Let's focus on page 3 of the Steven Strange comic for this. We have two characters, Steven and Martha, as well as backgrounds. We need to make a layer for each color that the characters have, and I find this easiest to manage if I make a layer folder for each character to store their color layers in. So that's our first step.

At the bottom of the **Layers** palette, click on the **New Layer Folder** icon three times to make three folders. Double click on each folder to rename it. Then we're going to set up layers inside each folder for the different parts of the character. I usually start with hair and skin first, and then move down to clothes. Make and rename your layers so that you have these set up.

 If you always have the same parts for a character, record this as an **Auto action** and play it to save time.

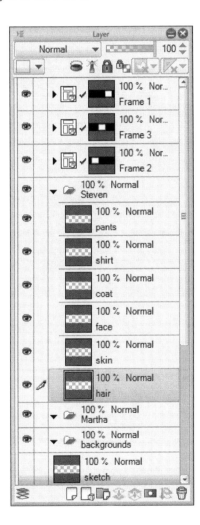

Do the same for any other characters that you have in your scene. Collapse any folders that you aren't currently working in so they aren't taking up valuable screen space.

Now take the **Auto select** tool, making sure that it's set to **Select Another Layer for reference** so that it will take into account the line art layers above your base color layers, and begin to fill in your base colors. If you remember back in *Chapter 7, Ready! Set! Action!*, we set the **Expand selection and fill with color** actions to key commands (shortcuts), so use those to fill your selections quickly.

We've got the base colors down (as shown in the preceding screenshot), but if you look closely you can see that some areas didn't get filled all the way. Take a close look at the folds on the shirt, and the tips of the hair and eyebrows and you'll see a bit of white space. We'll go back now and fill in the little white bits with the pen tool and our base color.

Can't see the white spaces? Double-click on the **Paper** layer to change the color and pick something bright. You'll be able to see bright orange or pink a lot better than white. Be sure to pick a color you aren't using already!

Changing the **Paper** layer color to something bright will also remind you to fill in any spaces that need to be white, such as eyes, teeth, or clothes, before you go painting in a background and realize that it's still transparent. Refer to the preceding screenshot.

Okay, now that we have our base colors laid down, we can get to shading and highlighting. Ready? Let's do it!

Coloring the hair

Just like putting down the base colors, I start with the hair first. Start wherever you feel comfortable, be it the skin, clothes, eyes, hair, whatever! Select the **hair** layer and then click on the Lock transparent pixels icon at the top of the layer palette as shown in the following screenshot:

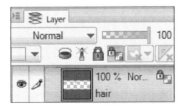

You can see in the preceding screenshot that there is now a little lock and a checkerboard to the right of the layer name, and that symbol matches the icon that we clicked, so our layer's transparent pixels will now not be affected. This means that only the pixels that we have already filled in will react to whatever we do. Just to see how this works, take your pen or pencil tool and drag a big scribble across your hair layer.

No matter what tool you pick, whether it be pencil, brush, or eraser, the space outside of your hair base color will not be drawn on so long as you have the transparent pixels locked as shown in the preceding screenshot.

Bonus

If you mess up, or don't like the way one part of your picture is coming out, and you have each section of base colors on their own layer, you can start over again easily. Either take a brush or a pen tool and go over the area that you want to set back to flat color, or use the **Edit | Fill** (*Alt* + *Del*) command to set the layer back to the base color.

The first step in shading the hair is to block out the darker areas with a soft edged brush having a color darker than the base color. Let's make such a custom brush to do the job.

Under the **Oil paint brush** sub tool I'm going to duplicate an existing tool by selecting it and then using the **Create copy of currently selected sub tool** icon in the **Sub tool** palette. It doesn't matter much which tool you copy because we'll be adjusting the settings anyway. Rename the tool and select an icon background color if you'd like as shown in the following screenshot:

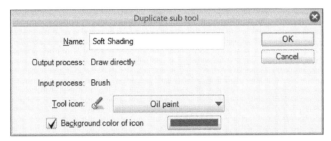

Now, open the **Sub tool detail** screen so that we can adjust the settings of our brush. We want to make sure this brush will be affected by the pressure of our stylus, so under the **Brush Size** make sure that the **Pen Pressure** checkbox is checked in the menu to the right of the brush size option.

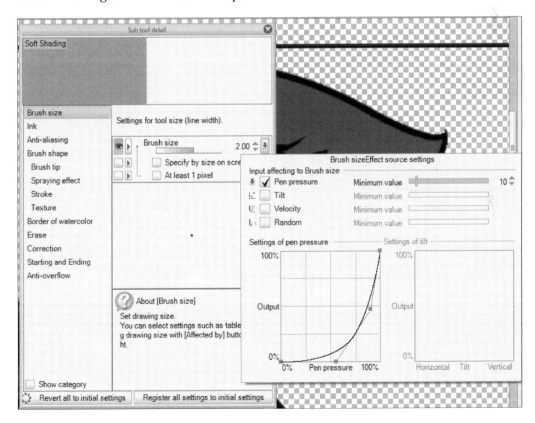

Next let's go to the **Ink** menu. Make sure that the opacity of your tool is set to **100%** and that the blending mode is **Normal**. We'll be using blending modes in a second, but with our soft brush we just want the exact color that we pick up for shading to be what's laid down by the brush. The **Mix ground color** option should also be deselected. Refer to the following screenshot:

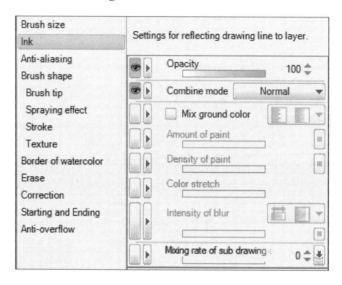

Now, under the **Brush tip** menu, change the tip shape from **Circle** to **Material**, and choose one or two Materials that have a soft, cloudy effect to them. The drop-down menu next to **Direction** on my **Soft shading** tool has the following options turned on as shown in the following screenshot:

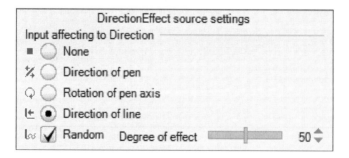

Under the dropdown, to the right of the **Brush density** setting, check the **Pen Pressure** option and keep the minimum value set to **0**.

Now the soft shading brush should be ready to use. Select a color darker than the base color for the hair and go over any areas that will be in shadow. Again, make sure to pay attention to any line weights for placement of shadows.

Don't worry too much if the shading is subtle. We're going to adjust it here in a moment with the secret weapon of this coloring style. (Refer to the preceding screenshot.) Are you ready?

Next we're going to use a combination of the **Lasso selection** tool and the **Gradient** tool to do further shading and highlighting on the hair. Select the **Gradient** tool (Shortcut G) and then select the **From drawing to transparent color** sub tool. What this does is it makes a gradient from the color that you have currently selected to transparent pixels, instead of making a gradient from white or any other color. We want this tool because we'll want our base color to still show.

In the **Tool property** palette, set the **Combine mode** to **Multiply**.

 You can create custom Gradation tools too! Since I use this coloring method a lot, I have Multiply (for shading) and Overlay (for highlighting) gradation tools set up in a custom tab. This way no time is wasted changing settings, the tool change is just a click away!

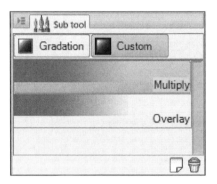

Now that we're ready with our **Gradient** tool, we can start selecting our shadow areas with the **Lasso selection** tool.

This works best if you select just a few areas at one time. Since we're going to drag a gradient over the Lasso selection, working in smaller chunks is better right now. If we were to select each shadow that we wanted to add to the hair at once, and then drag out our gradient, we would get something like this:

The right side of the hair is very, very dark with hardly any gradient at all, while the left side of the hair is barely shaded. So that's why we'll work in smaller selection areas. Let's start with just the right side of the hair.

Use the **Lasso selection** tool to select your darker areas. Don't worry about being perfect outside of the line art. Because we still have the transparent pixels locked, hence the **Gradient** tool will only affect our base color anyway, so don't waste time trying to get the selection perfect. Make sure that it does go under the line work, though, so that there isn't a halo effect around the edges of the color.

Also, do not go over the entire soft shading area that you had already laid down. We want some of this shading to still show when we're done, so try to make your selections a little smaller than the rough shadows that you've already blocked out. Refer to the following screenshot:

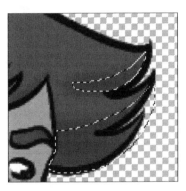

Now take the **Multiply** gradient tool and drag a gradient out, starting in the area that will be the darkest and ending in the area that will be the lightest. (Drag towards the light source, not away from it!) Refer to the following screenshot:

This will give you some shadows with hard edges, and some that fade and become soft. This is exactly what we want. Now, continue with the rest of the shadows, selecting small areas and then going over them with the **Drawing Color to Transparent** gradient set to the **Multiply combine** mode. We'll have a result as shown in the following screenshot:

 While shading and highlighting hair, don't be afraid to make "jagged" selections that zig zag back and forth. This will make the hair look more like it has locks and strands instead of being a flat shape.

Now to add highlights! Select a color, which is lighter than your base color and change your **Gradient** tool to the **Overlay combine** mode. The color that you choose will depend on the color of your character's hair. For red and brown hair I usually like to highlight with orange or yellow. Blond hair is usually highlighted with white. And black hair is usually highlighted with light blue and then white for extra shine.

In the following screenshot, I've included a few examples of different color schemes for hair. Red/brown shaded with purple and yellow, blonde shaded with orange, blonde shaded with brown, and black shaded with blue and white.

I obviously don't know everything there is to know about color and color theory. Heck, I won't even claim to know more than a mediocre amount about color and color theory! Color is a harsh mistress, and the study of color is a long and tedious process for most of us. But this is what works for me for most characters. I urge you to read coloring tutorials and painting tutorials though, to learn more about how to combine colors and the different moods that color evokes.

Alright, back to our comic panel. Select a highlight color and use the **Lasso selection** tool to mark out areas that your light source is hitting. Then use the **Overlay** gradient to make your highlights.

[If you don't like the way the highlights look, try changing from **Overlay blending** mode to **Screen**.]

To bring a little detail back into the dark areas, I sometimes add a thin bit of the highlight color, right on the edge of the shadows, as you can see in the hair on the right side of the following screenshot:

To make the hair look even shinier, we can add white highlights inside of the highlights that we've already put on the image. You can even make them very subtle by starting your gradient farther away from the edge of the selection area, as I've done with the white highlights on the top of the hair here as shown in the following screenshot:

Save your work so far.

Coloring the skin

Now we're ready to move on to the skin portions of our character. Select the layer with your skin base colors and make sure that the Lock transparent pixel icon has been selected so that only our colored areas are active. Then, just like with our hair, go ahead and get a darker shade and go over the areas that will be in shadow. Don't forget inside the ear, under the brows, and underneath the chin—depending on your light source. Also don't forget to shade any other areas of skin that might not be in view when you're zoomed in, such as the hands or legs. Trust me, it's just easier to do all the skin at once than to try going back and finding the color you shaded the face with, so that the color on the hands match! Refer to the following screenshot:

Now, with the same shading color, use the **Lasso selection** tool and start making selections on the shadowed areas. I usually start with the biggest areas first, which in this case are the right side of the face and under the chin. Select each of these areas and add a **Multiply blending** mode gradient to each individually. Then darken the other shaded areas, adding detail to the neck and the contours of the face as needed.

One of the reasons why I love this coloring method so much is that it saves time. Need a shadow darker and deeper? Just make a smaller selection and go over it with the same gradient again. Because the tool is set to **Multiply** and so the color will continue to get darker with each application. You can see that I did additional shading under the neck, on the side of the face, and inside of the ear to get these deeper shadows and add shape as shown in the following screenshot:

Now using your highlight color and the **Gradient** tool set to **Overlay** and mark out the light areas of your skin. If you get any areas while you're coloring that you don't like the look of, by the way, you can adjust them some using either the **Color Mixing** or **Blur** tools. Let's say we don't like the very hard look of the highlight on the nose here. Refer to the following screenshot:

Simply run the **Color mixing** tool over the edge of the highlight to reshape and soften it as shown in the following screenshot:

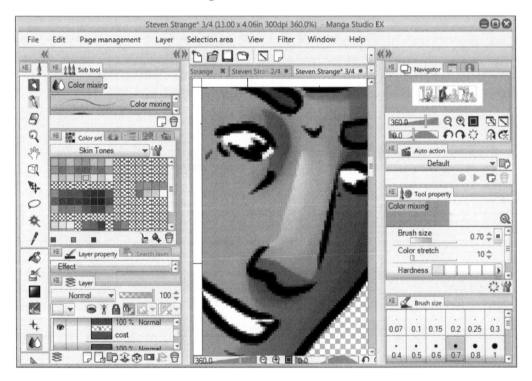

Continue adding light until you like the results. Also, try adding a little light back into the shaded areas, such as on the cheek, to add a bit more dimension to the facial features as shown in the following screenshot:

Now use the same process for the coat, shirt, and jeans. Lock the transparent pixels of the layer, use the soft shading brush to block out the shadows, and then use the **Lasso selection** and **Gradient** tools to add deeper shading and highlights. I find that clothes can sometimes get away with having a little less contrast between the base color and highlight, unless they are supposed to be a shiny fabric or synthetic leather as shown in the following screenshot:

Now we can use the same process on any other characters in the scene. I like to color my characters before doing the backgrounds, but I know a lot of people who prefer exactly the opposite too. Refer to the following screenshot:

Save your work, just in case something happens!

Backgrounds and you

This same method of coloring outlined in the preceding paragraph can be used for backgrounds, cars, or anything that you want—if you want! But I personally prefer to do a little more of a painterly approach on my backgrounds. To me, it makes the characters stand out a bit more. So here's how I do my backgrounds for my comics.

First of all, make a layer for the background. Then use the rectangle marquee to drag out a selection of the entire length and width of the panel. Then use the gradient tool and fill in the selection with the basic color that you want for the background. In this case I'm going with a dingy yellow-green sort of color for our police station as shown in the following screenshot:

Note that the lighter part of the gradient is on the side of the image with the light source.

Let's take care of the desk first, because it's the largest element of the background other than the wall that's behind it. Plus it has the most little details on it, so if we get it out of the way first, it will be done!

Grab the **Polyline selection** tool and select the desk area. Just do the entire area, because as long as this layer is behind the colors for your characters then it won't matter if you go over their arm or hands, and we'll fill in the papers and other things on the desk once we're done with the desk itself. Once you've made the selection, fill in the desk with a brown color as shown in the following screenshot:

Now, we're going to take one of the natural media paint brushes and shade the desk with it. The brushes that I like the best for doing this are the ones that I didn't make. However, you can download them from fellow artist and incredible comic-maker Julie Devin Minter's site at `http://monstersoupcomic.com/manga-studio-5-brushes/`.

If you prefer to make your own brushes rather than downloading them, though, here are the **Mix ground color** settings for the brush that I will be using in this section, shown in the following screenshot:

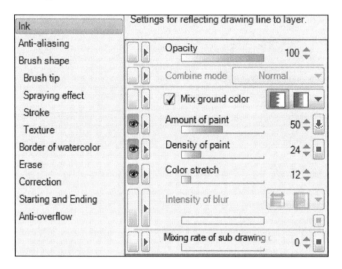

Leave the selection as active around the area that you're going to paint. Then take lighter and darker browns, yellows, and even reds and purples to make the highlights and shadows on the desk. Make sure to keep in mind the places where the items on the desk would be causing shadows. For the time being I have left the objects on the desk pad without cast shadows because we will paint those once we work on the desk pad. No sense in painting on those shadows if we'll just have to do them again!

Be sure to add some little details, too. We can take a dark color and a small brush and add hints of wood grain on parts of the desk to make it just a bit more realistic.

Refer to the following screenshot:

Next we can do the pad that's present at the center of the desk. Deselect the desk area and use the **Polyline selection** tool to select the pad area. Fill it with a color—how about blue? And then shade and put some lighter areas on it too.

You can also use a textured brush to add speckling, making it look as though the desk pad is made of slightly fuzzy cloth. Refer to the following screenshot:

Now continue using the same process for the other pieces of the background. Save time by painting like colored objects, such as the bits of paper on the desk, all at the same time. To select more than one area at a time, either hold down *Shift* while making your selection, or ensure that the Select Additionally icon under the **Tool Property** panel for the Polyline selection is on. After you are done, the desk pad will look as shown in the following screenshot:

You can either select the smaller objects too in order to color them, or make your brush very small and just try not to go out of the inks. I find this method to be faster for tiny areas rather than spending time selecting them.

Finish up the desk and now we can do the same thing for the chair that Martha is sitting on. Since it's not much inside the frame, and mostly covered by the character and the word balloon, it won't take much effort to do. Fill with brown and then add some shading to it just so that it doesn't look flat.

Lastly, we can add some texture to the back wall and make it look more like a wallpaper. Select a color slightly darker than the dark section of your background gradient and just apply a little bit of texture. You shouldn't need much!

We can also adjust the word balloon tail since it's not really pointing at Steven, and it should be since he's the one speaking in this frame. You can edit an existing word balloon by double-clicking on it with the **Object selection** sub tool. Select the tail in this way and you can manipulate the control points by left-clicking them and dragging. Hitting *Delete* will get rid of the tail and then you can draw a new one if you wish. The end result will be as shown in the following screenshot:

Special effects

When you're making your comics, you may come across coloring situations that I usually call special effects. Things such as shiny/reflective objects, magic or special powers, and using photographic patterns require special effects. We'll see how I handle these special instances, and then you can develop your own technique if mine doesn't work for you!

Shine

Let's start with a circle drawn on a transparent canvas. We're going to take this circle and turn it in to a ball bearing. On a new layer under the line for the circle, fill with a flat medium gray color as shown in the following screenshot:

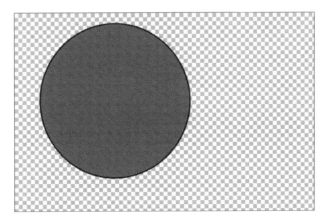

Lock the transparent pixel for this layer and take your soft shading brush. Using a dark gray, add a shadow to the right side of the sphere, but do not add it all the way to the edge of it! Leave some of the base color between the shadow and the line. Then use the **Lasso selection** tool and the **Multiply** gradient to add some darker shadows. The end result will be as shown in the following screenshot:

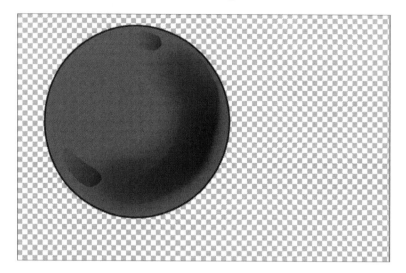

Our ball bearing is going to be sitting on a piece of blue paper, so we'll need to add some blue to the coloring to show that it's reflecting the blue of the paper. Select a light blue color and use the **Lasso selection** tool and the **Overlay** gradient to add a strip of blue to the right side of the sphere, and to the highlight area as well. The end result will be as shown in the following screenshot:

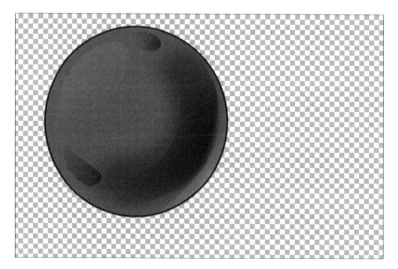

Because this is supposed to be shiny, I would like to add a little extra highlight. Take the soft shading brush and some white, and go very lightly over the highlight area with it first. Then use the **Lasso selection** tool and the **Overlay** gradient to add a few spots of light over the soft shading. The end result will be as shown in the following screenshot:

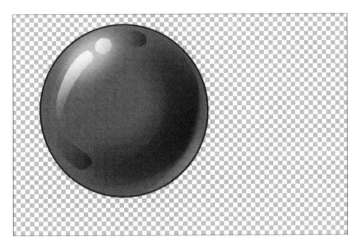

Create a layer beneath the color layers for the sphere and use the **polyline selection** to add a blue polygon shape for our paper. Then use the **ellipse** selection tool and multiply the gradient to add a cast shadow on to the paper. The end result will be as shown in the following screenshot:

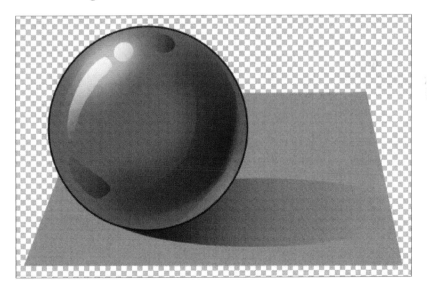

Now, what if we want to make our sphere look extra shiny? Easily done. First, let's create a layer behind the paper though and fill it with a dark color so we can see the effect that we're about to do. By the way, this effect looks good on hair, too, if you use it sparingly.

Create a layer above the line art and set it to the **Screen combine** mode. Now take white color and your soft shading brush and go over the highlighted area and some of the line, making them brighter. You can also add a little bit of this down in the reflected blue area on the shadow side too. The end result will be as shown in the following screenshot:

This same basic principle can be applied to many different shiny surfaces. Here are a few examples of pieces where I've used this same technique.

For flat, shiny objects use the **polyline selection** tool and alternate random dark and light shapes, like I've done on the sword and the brooch, as shown in the following screenshot:

Note that on the sword, especially, there are hints of blue and red in the metal picked up from the coat. I've found this to be a handy trick to making something look convincing as metal.

Using photographic patterns

Back in *Chapter 5*, *Living in a Material World*, we went over how to create pattern materials and use them. But what if you have a photograph of a pattern that you'd like to incorporate into your illustration? To show you how to do this, we'll be adding a wooden floor underneath a character in the next exercise.

Pick an image of a character that you like and which you can get on to a transparent canvas. Use the **rectangle selection** tool to make a floor area and fill it with brown. Then use the **Edit | Transform | Free Transform** option to bring the corners of the rectangle in some, making a floor in perspective. Once you're happy with the shape of your floor, hit *Enter*.

Then we need to add our pattern image. You can find lots of stock images and patterns on sites like `DeviantArt.com` just by doing a search. Be sure to read any terms of use that the owner of the pattern may have, and ask permission before doing anything commercial with their texture unless they say that it's free to use.

Once you've gotten a texture for your floor, go to **File | Import | Pattern from image**. Navigate to your file and click on **Open**. Refer to the following screenshot:

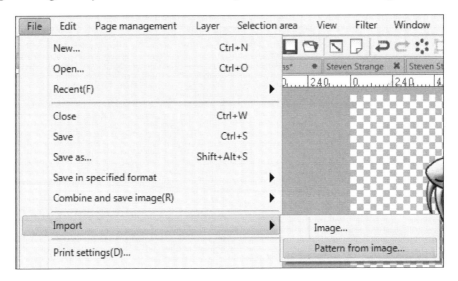

When you import your image, it will appear on a layer by itself with a blue bounding box. Use the bounding box to resize your pattern if you'd like. Then right-click on the texture layer and under **Layer Settings** click on the **Clip at layer below** option. This will restrict the pattern to show just on the brown floor shape that we made a moment ago. The result of this is shown in-the following screenshot:

Alright, we have the wood texture, but it still looks very flat and not in perspective like the rest of the floor, right? The character can't stand on a floor that's vertical (unless they have a super-power that allows that, of course!), so we need to adjust the texture the same way that we adjust the fill color. Right-click on the texture layer and select **Rasterize**. This will allow us to use the same **Free Transform** tool that we used earlier. Adjust the pattern so that it's skewed more in line with the shape of the floor. Refer to the following screenshot:

Now, in order to change the effect that the pattern has on the color of the floor, all you have to do is change the **Combine Mode** of the pattern layer. Try out a few and notice how they change the look and color of the floor. I decided on the **Darken** option for my floor because it seemed to work best with the photo and base brown color.

Next, add a layer above the pattern and add some shadows and highlights, especially under the character so that it looks like they're actually standing on the floor. Use a soft brush and blur the shadow edges. Then drop the opacity of the layer a little so that the pattern on the floor comes through as shown in the following screenshot:

Reflections

Doing a reflection on a shiny floor, pane of glass, or even water isn't too difficult. Again, I'll show you my method and if it doesn't work for you feel free to change anything about it to better suit your needs!

The first thing to do is to make a copy of the line art and coloring for the character or object that is being reflected. In this case, I'm taking the martial arts character from the previous section and adding a reflection to the floor. Make copies of the ink layer and all the coloring layers and merge them down in to a copy of the entire character as the first step. Refer to the following screenshot:

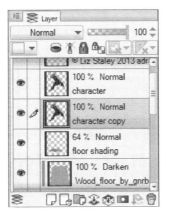

Now, with your copy layer selected, go to **Edit | Transform | Reverse Vertically**. You will end up with something like the following screenshot:

Use the **Move Layer** tool to drag the reversed copy down so that the character's feet are aligned, the same way that they would be if the floor was actually reflecting them.

Now you can adjust the opacity and the **Combine mode** until you find settings that you like. The image that I created is using the **Overlay** combine mode and **60% opacity**. Take a soft-edged eraser and go lightly over the reflection to make it blend in spots, depending on how reflective your surface is. Your reflection is now done!

Summary

Alright, you Master of Manga Studio! You've come to the end of the finishing touches chapter. I hope with some ideas for your own techniques, and with some tips on how to fly through your toning and coloring you are working even faster and more efficiently than before.

In this chapter we learned about:

- Creating screentones using the **Simple Tone** menu
- Saving tones to the **Materials** palette
- Using tones from the **Materials** palette
- Making a custom soft-edged shading brush
- Coloring in the comic book style using the **Lasso selection** tool and **Gradient** tools
- Painting backgrounds
- Creating special effects like reflections, adding patterns, and shiny surfaces

Recommended Reading

I have decided to include here a list of books that I've found very helpful over the years as an artist and writer. This is by no means a definitive list of helpful books on the subjects, but they are ones that I have read and enjoyed. They include:

- *Drawing on the Right Side of the Brain, Betty Edwards*
- *The Artist's Way: A Spiritual Path to Higher Creativity, Julia Cameron*
- *Making Comics: Storytelling Secrets of Comics, Manga, and Graphic Novels, Scott McCloud*
- *How to Make Webcomics, Brad Guigar, Dave Kellett, Scott Kurtz,* and *Kris Straub*
- *How to Draw Noir Comics: The art and technique of visual storytelling, Shawn Martinbrough*
- *Dynamic Figure Drawing, Burne Hogarth*
- *Dynamic Light and Shade, Burne Hogarth*
- *Dynamic Wrinkles and Drapery, Burne Hogarth*
- *Drawing Dynamic Hands, Burne Hogarth*
- *Anatomy and Drawing, Victor Perard*
- *How to Draw Manga: Illustrating Battles, Hikaru Hayashi*
- *Vanishing Point: Perspective for Comics from the Ground Up, Jason Cheeseman-Meyer*
- *The Comic Artist's Photo Reference Collections, Buddy Scalera*
- *The DC Comic's Guide to Writing Comics, Dennis O'Neil*
- *Alan Moore's Writing for Comics, Alan Moore*
- *Invisible Ink: A practical guide to building stories that resonate, Brian McDonald*
- *Save the Cat! The last book on screenwriting you'll ever need, Blake Snyder*

Helpful websites

- `DeviantArt.com`: Tutorials, textures, and helpful application resources a click away

- `PoseManiacs.com`: 3D poses of all types, in different angles, able to be rotated

- `Fineart.sk`: Andrew Loomis Anatomy books and other anatomy references

- `Posespace.com/posetool`: Collection of models in poses, searchable by gender, props, clothing, and more

- `Scott-Eaton.com/category/bodies-in-motion`: Images of the human form in motion

- `Ctrlpaint.com`: Free digital painting classes

- `Pinterest.com/characterdesigh`: Character design references, lots of different ages, genders, and styles

Podcasts to listen to while working

- `PaperWingsPodcast.com`: A podcast by Chris Oatley and Lorra Innes, with the goal of helping elevate comics and inspire creators

- `WebcomicAlliance.com`: Podcasts and articles about everything from art to the business of comics

- `ww.libsyn.com` (Webcomics Weekly): Legendary creators Brad Guigar, Dave Kellett, Scott Kurtz, and Kris Straub dish out about various comic topics. Archive, no new episodes since November 2012

- `TGTMedia.com`: Kurt Sasso interviews creators in comics, film, game design, shows, and more. Large archive of interesting interviews!

- `ComicDish.com` (The Dish): The official podcast of the ComicDish hosting services, the free comic host with no ads!

Final thoughts

I thought I would end this book with a few words of wisdom that I've gathered over a lifetime of being an artist, and half a decade (so far) of being a comic creator.

No matter what you do, or what you create, there will always be people who don't like it.

You can be the best artist or storyteller in the world, and there will always be people out there who don't agree with what you do. They won't like the way you write dialog, or the way that you draw exactly five eyelashes on each character. They'll think you're an overrated hack who doesn't deserve anyone looking at their art.

Don't listen to these people. Even Einstein had people who thought he was stupid and crazy. If you persist, eventually you will reach your definition of success.

Never stop learning.

No matter how much you've improved, you can still learn more. Got faces down but still can't do hands? Look at tutorials and do tons of hand drawings. Pick one or two things at a time that you feel you could do better at and focus on those things until you're better. Study the work of those who inspire you. If the artists that you admire have YouTube channels or Deviant Art accounts, follow them. Ask them about their technique; ask if they're willing to help other artists or if they'll do tutorials on something that you like in their work. Most artists are more than willing to help out others and share their knowledge.

I love to watch creative work of others, because this helps me to learn something new. Whether it's a new way to ink or a way to use a layer combine mode to make an effect, you can always pick up at least one thing from watching someone else.

Just remember, if you're in person and you want to watch an artist draw, ask if it's okay first! A lot of artists get nervous when people watch them. (If you ever meet me at a convention though and want to watch me draw, that's okay. I don't mind it!)

Make what you would love to see and read.

If you have a comic idea that will be the next Penny Arcade, but you don't like playing video games, don't make a video game comic. If you like to draw cartoon animals but think that Manga style will get more attention, don't draw Manga style. Your passion will come through in your work, and if you don't love what you're doing then it will show!

I don't play a lot of video games, so doing a video game comic wouldn't be right for me. However, I love old cartoons — the cheesier the better — and I love giant robots and science fiction. So I decided to make a comic that combined these things. If I tried to do a comic about gamers, I'd be calling it in most of the time and it would show, trust me. Like Hanna-Barbera style cartoons? Analyze what you like about them and incorporate it into your work. Don't draw Manga just because it's "in."

Find a way to forget hurtful things and remember the good things.

In his interview on TGT Media, Michael "Mookie" Terracciano said something that I will never forget. He pointed out that, being a comic creator and going to, say, a convention, you could spend all weekend with people coming up to you and telling you how much they love your work. And then one person could come up and tell you that you are the worst artist on the planet and you will remember that one person for the rest of your life and forget all the compliments that you received.

This isn't just something that artists and writers do, either. It's something that all people do. And having it pointed out really made me think hard, and I came up with a system for me that allows me to remember the good things that have been said to me. I'm going to share it with you, in the hopes that you'll create something that works for you if you have trouble with remembering your compliments.

I started up a file where I store the nice things that are said about me, whether it's someone thanking me for help on Twitter or telling me that they enjoyed the way I drew a panel, I save them. And then when I'm feeling bad about myself or like everyone is against me, I open that file and realize that things aren't so bad as they seem. I have the proof right in front of me.

Be careful which critiques you listen to, and which you ignore.

Critique is an important part of being a craftsperson and improving at it. Artists of all types need critique to know where they need to improve and what they could be focusing on. If you don't know that you keep drawing hands on backwards, you'll do it over and over again and it will be hard to stop! Or if your coloring is flat and needs some life breathed into it with more contrast, having someone point that out can steer you in the right direction for making improvements. We need to know what we could improve on so that we can focus on the problem areas.

But not all critique is the same. Get to know your comfort level with critique. Personally, I'm a little delicate sometimes so I choose not to seek out some of the more "hard-core" critique sites and instead like to ask for help via my Facebook and DeviantArt pages. This is because I can get advice from people that I trust who aren't going to tear me down just to do it.

The Internet can be a hard place to post your creativity to. It's like sharing your soul and your heart with someone and having them rip it out when they say something bad about it. So, while you should listen to critiques, make sure that you listen to the critiques that are right for you.

Don't be afraid to experiment; even when you think you have a style or technique perfected, be willing to tweak it and test if there's a better way.

Experimentation is the spice of life, or something like that. Do something that you've never done before once in awhile. Make your line art dark blue or brown instead of black. Use a watercolor brush to paint a scene. Do some speed paintings of environments, or make characters by designing their silhouettes first. Browse a tutorial site and read any lessons that look interesting. Try different colorings of light on a character, draw a scene at night and paint it in nothing but purple and blue. Use a new brush to ink with. Create a new pencil tool. Try your hand at some calligraphy.

Whatever new things you can test out, do it! You'll discover what you're good at and what you're terrible at, and you'll start to learn new things that you can apply to what you love already.

If it doesn't work for you, don't do it.

Some people will tell you to create every day, even if you don't want to. Some people will tell you that not creating every day is fine, because you need to recharge your batteries sometimes. The thing is that, if a method doesn't work for you, you shouldn't attempt to use it.

You could learn the secret to the best coloring technique in the world, but if you hate the results or the process then you aren't going to love using it. You could download the best set of custom brushes on the entire Internet, but if you don't want an oil painting look to your work, you won't use them. So, simply, if it doesn't work for you then don't do it. Give new things a try all the time, but if you find that after you've tried them you don't like them, don't continue with them.

And finally...

Have fun, and enjoy everything that Manga Studio has to offer your creative process! I've had a great time guiding you through the program and working together, and I hope that you have too!

Index

H

hair
  coloring, in comic book style 241-249
Highlight layer 129
Horizontalize eye level option 194

I

image
  finishing, materials used 130-132
inking 221-225
inking pen
  creating 40-44
Ink menu
  combine mode 53
  Mix ground color menu 53
  opacity 52

K

keyboard shortcuts
  setting 182

L

Lasso selection tool 245
layer below option 122
Layer Mask option 175
left-handed setup
  for on-screen drawing tablets 92, 93
  for regular tablets 89-91
left-handed setups 88
Ligne Claire 223
Linear option 208
Linear sub tool 196
line art
  creating, from photo 177-180
Line Weight principle 223

M

Manga Studio
  about 65
  screen elements 80, 81
Manga Studio 5 7, 95
Material option 37, 42

Material Property window 109
materials
  editing 108-117
  searching 102-108
  used, for image finishing 130-132
  used, for laying out frames 213-216
Materials option 39
Materials palette 217, 218
Materials tab 101
Materials window
  3D 103
  about 102, 103
  Color pattern 102
  Image material 103
  Manga material 102
  Monochromic pattern 102
Mesh Transform tools 131
millimeters (MM) 91
Mix color 69
Mix ground color menu 53
model
  importing 160-162
  positioning 140-142

O

Object selection tool 187, 202, 209
Object Select tool 214
on-screen drawing tablets
  left-handed setup 92, 93
opacity 52

P

Page Manager tab 7
pages
  navigating 14-16
  rearranging 14-16
paintbrush
  used, for painting 45-49
painting
  with custom paintbrush 45-49
palette windows
  moving 79-86
Paper Color option 124
PaperWingsPodcast.com 272

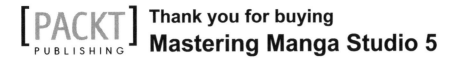

Thank you for buying
Mastering Manga Studio 5

About Packt Publishing

Packt, pronounced 'packed', published its first book "*Mastering phpMyAdmin for Effective MySQL Management*" in April 2004 and subsequently continued to specialize in publishing highly focused books on specific technologies and solutions.

Our books and publications share the experiences of your fellow IT professionals in adapting and customizing today's systems, applications, and frameworks. Our solution based books give you the knowledge and power to customize the software and technologies you're using to get the job done. Packt books are more specific and less general than the IT books you have seen in the past. Our unique business model allows us to bring you more focused information, giving you more of what you need to know, and less of what you don't.

Packt is a modern, yet unique publishing company, which focuses on producing quality, cutting-edge books for communities of developers, administrators, and newbies alike. For more information, please visit our website: www.packtpub.com.

Writing for Packt

We welcome all inquiries from people who are interested in authoring. Book proposals should be sent to author@packtpub.com. If your book idea is still at an early stage and you would like to discuss it first before writing a formal book proposal, contact us; one of our commissioning editors will get in touch with you.

We're not just looking for published authors; if you have strong technical skills but no writing experience, our experienced editors can help you develop a writing career, or simply get some additional reward for your expertise.

Unity 3.x Scripting

ISBN: 978-1-849692-30-4   Paperback: 292 pages

Write efficient, reusable scripts to build custom characters, game environments, and control enemy AI in your Unity game

1. Make your characters interact with buttons and program triggered action sequences

2. Create custom characters and code dynamic objects and players' interaction with them

3. Synchronize movement of character and environmental objects

4. Add and control animations to new and existing characters

Blender 2.5 Character Animation Cookbook

ISBN: 978-1-849513-20-3   Paperback: 308 pages

50 great recipes for giving soul to your characters by building high-quality rigs and understanding the principles of movement

1. Learn how to create efficient and easy to use character rigs

2. Understand and make your characters , so that your audience believes they're alive

3. See common approaches when animating your characters in real world situations

4. Learn the techniques needed to achieve various setups, from IK-FK blending to corrective shape keys and eyes controllers

Please check **www.PacktPub.com** for information on our titles

Cinema 4D R13 Cookbook

ISBN: 978-1-849691-86-4   Paperback: 514 pages

Design, develop, and deploy feature-rich PHP web applications with this MVC framework

1. Master all the important aspects of Cinema 4D

2. Learn how real-world knowledge of cameras and lighting translates onto a 3D canvas

3. Learn Advanced features like Mograph, Xpresso, and Dynamics.

4. Become an advanced Cinema 4D user with concise and effective recipes

Papervision3D Essentials

ISBN: 978-1-847195-72-2   Paperback: 428 pages

Create interactive Papervision3D applications with stunning effects and powerful animations

1. Build stunning, interactive Papervision3D applications from scratch

2. Export and import 3D models from Autodesk 3ds Max, SketchUp and Blender to Papervision3D

3. In-depth coverage of important 3D concepts with demo applications, screenshots and example code

4. Step-by-step guide for beginners and professionals with tips and tricks based on the authors' practical experience

Please check **www.PacktPub.com** for information on our titles

Printed in Great Britain
by Amazon